Historic Churches
and Temples of Georgia

Historic Churches

and Temples of Georgia

A Book of Watercolors and Drawings

by Gloria Sampson

with an introduction by James Patrick

MERCER
UNIVERSITY PRESS

ISBN 0-86554-242-2

The paper used in this publication meets
the minimum requirements of American National Standard
for Information Sciences—Permanence of Paper
for Printed Library Materials, ANSI Z39.48-1984.

Library of Congress Cataloging-in-Publication Data

Sampson, Gloria, 1940–
Historic churches and temples of Georgia

1. Georgia—Church history.   2. Judaism—Georgia—History.
3. Churches—Georgia.   4. Synagogues—Georgia.   I. Title.
BR555.G4S26   1987   280'.09758   86-31116
ISBN 0-86554-242-2 (alk. paper)

Contents

This book is dedicated
to my husband

LLOYD BRENT SAMPSON

and to my mother

MARIE ROSE JONES

in appreciation

Preface

My interest in drawing and in the out-of-doors developed quite naturally when I was a child growing up in Montana and Alaska. I attended the California College of Arts and Crafts, a small private art school in Oakland, California. Although my major was interior design, I was equally interested in fine art and architecture. Since many of my art classes were on location in the older sections of the city, I found myself increasingly drawn to the ornate Victorian houses for which the San Francisco area is famous. After graduation I continued to haunt the same areas, painting and drawing my favorite subjects. As more and more of these structures disappeared in the name of urban renewal, to make room for new construction or freeways, I began to realize that paintings such as mine were an important way of keeping these irreplaceable buildings alive. Thus began my interest in historic preservation.

Moving from California to Georgia was an easy transition artistically, as I continued to paint out-of-doors during numerous journeys around the state. I soon began painting many charming rural and urban churches and their cemeteries. As the stack of paintings grew, so did my interest in the history of the churches, and the integral part they played in the development of Georgia. A natural consequence of this interest was a full-length book depicting both the architecture and the evolution of many of the most significant houses of worship in Georgia.

As much as possible, the houses of worship in the book are evenly distributed, both by location and denomination. Although it would be impossible for a book of this size to contain every one of Georgia's historical churches and temples, this one offers a choice selection of them, from the great Catholic cathedrals with their marble statues and gold leaf to the one-room rural churches built of logs or clapboard.

Generally, I selected the churches and temples that are included because of their relationship to the development of Georgia or because of their architectural significance or both. My sources for finding information about the various churches included the National Register of Historic Places, Georgia Historical Markers, local libraries and historical societies, word of mouth, and luck.

Acknowledgments

If, before I had begun this book, someone had sat me down and described in detail what would be involved in its creation, I would have been somewhat overwhelmed and intimidated. Fortunately, no one did. When obstacles did become apparent, someone always seemed to appear to help me along.

My friends at the Historic Columbus Foundation, especially Janice Biggers and Clason Kyle were enthusiastic and supportive the day I told them about my idea and presented them with a "stack" of watercolors of churches. Janice Hardy from the Art Department of Georgia College in Milledgeville steered me directly to Mercer University Press in Macon for an interview, and the publishers seemed very receptive to the idea of the book. It was a good beginning.

Dr. Elizabeth Lyon and her staff from the Georgia Department of Natural Resources Historic Preservation office in Atlanta supplied me with a complete listing of properties on the National Register and other information for "finding churches." Dr. Joseph Mahan was my verbal contact for ferreting them out around Columbus and South Georgia. The network of historical societies scattered across the state made a wealth of information available. I offer special thanks to Becky Gaddis, Laurens County Historical Society; Bob Davis, Marble Valley Historical Society; Tom Hill, Historic Thomasville Foundation; E. H. Armor, Greene County historian; Matthew Moye of Westville; and Dan Biggers, director of the Martha Berry Museum.

Librarians were most helpful, and one could get lost for days in the well-stocked libraries of the Atlanta Historical Society and the Georgia Historical Society in Savannah. Ann Smith was particularly helpful in burrowing through files to find a few elusive churches that are listed on the National Register and located in Chatham County— somewhere! Brady Wilson from the Bradley Library in Columbus, Caroline Anglin of Parks Memorial Library in Richland, Emily Anthony of the Northeast Regional Library in Clarkesville, and the librarian from Lake Blacksheer Library in Americus were all instrumental in helping me to compile the information about these buildings.

Many thanks to the clergymen from all of the churches and temples included, along with church historians and secretaries who willingly took their time to give me guided tours and shared both written and verbal history with me. Marion Towns from Mountville is one of those people.

Approximately one hundred ten churches from around the state are represented in the book, and so many individuals are responsible for their inclusion in so many different ways that I cannot possibly mention them all, but I shall try. Without the carefully written directions from Nell Thompson in Sylvester I would never have found Old Mount Horeb Baptist Church. Nancy Kitchens offered similar help to locate Richland Baptist Church. The enthusiasm Sambo Wilder has for Church Row in Louvale and historic preservation in her area, along with her appreciation for my work, have been an inspiration. Thanks to Beth Wood from Americus, who took me on a tour of the woods where Brother Lawrence's St. James Pennington Church once stood. The little log cabin church is now a part of the Andersonville Historic Site. Thanks to my longtime friend Lynn Barry, who introduced me to several wonderful churches which are represented in the book. She helped find an apartment in Savannah for my six-week stay there while working on chapter one. While working on chapter three, I was fortunate to house-sit for her and her family in their lovely Atlanta home. Thanks to my newly found friend and neighbor in Savannah, Ann Beeler, for leading me to helpful information through the historical society there. Thanks to Tommy Barnes for showing me the churches in Schley County, and to my friend Merry Tipton for loaning me her books about the Georgia Coast and enlightening me about the Darien area.

Special thanks to Caroline Kemp, who cheerfully typed and retyped the text and related work for this book, and to Joe Maher, who carefully transported the paintings a chapter at a time to photograph them expertly for the book.

Most of all, I want to thank my husband, Lloyd Sampson, who helped gather information while on location and who carefully and methodically sorted through file folders bulging with my research data in an attempt to decipher words, to eliminate verbiage, and to turn it all into an interesting, understandable text. He helped in every way possible with so many mundane details, from keeping the cars in good running order to making hotel reservations, so that I could paint.

I apologize for the many churches that were not included, but should have been.

Introduction

Drawing and architecture are indissolubly married. Architects must draw in order to discover the building that lies hidden in imagination until the pencil calls it out. Then they must draw in another way to produce the perspectives that convince the client, and in yet another to produce the system of technical notations that allows wood, stone, and steel to be assembled into the building they envision. Sometimes the process is foreshortened, the owner's sketch or the housecarpenter's hasty drawing replacing renderings and blueprints, but drawing there must be, or architecture will never exist. Once built, architecture belongs to the world, and as part of landscape or cityscape can be drawn by anyone who sees it. This drawing of buildings, whether as background or subject, has been important in European art since the Renaissance, from Canaletto to John Betjeman.

Why artists, who have the world before them, so often draw buildings or make them part of their art is not hard to discover. Throughout our lives buildings are our companions, mirrors of the beauty and meaning of the human scene, mute witnesses to worlds that were. As such they have an interest proper to the great art which, of all the arts, alone transforms place, stamping it with the human image of design. But artists do not paint because they remember or wish to record, but because the artist has seen something that must be explored and known. In pursuing a love affair with the knowable, the artist shows us what he or she has seen, and what he or she sees is more than texture, line, color, and form. It is one of the mysteries of art that the representation of the artist, often imprecise, sometimes deliberately distorted, tells us more than photographs and more than measured drawings. Drawing is an art of essences, photography an art of surfaces. Photographers must labor with light, viewpoint, and technique to accomplish with difficulty what the pencil or the brush can bring before us with a line. The pencil goes to the heart of the thing, and displays openly that inner reality the artist has seen. Van Gogh's peach blossoms show us a glory we might have missed, and Piranesi's stylus depicts his city with a depth and poignancy that historical texts can only shadow.

Artists paint and draw because they want to see. Sometimes, as in *Historic Churches and Temples of Georgia*, an artist develops a love affair with a kind of building, and enables us to share what she has seen. That we have not really seen these buildings is fairly certain. They stand on city streets, on clay hillsides and in groves that break the sweep of fields. But as a type of building having a distinctive significance, Georgia's churches are, through neglect born partly of familiarity, partly of forgetfulness, largely invisible. In making them visible, Gloria Sampson tells us something of ourselves, Georgia, and the American South.

The buildings she depicts are not always the stylish examples around which architectural histories are usually written. Georgia does have its stylish church buildings. Savannah's Independent Presbyterian Church, designed by John Holden Greene of Rhode Island and completed in 1819, shares with St. Philip's, Charleston, the place of honor among the Southern descendants of the stylish London churches (notably St.-Martin-in-the-Fields) of the eighteenth century. St. Paul's, Augusta, had distinguished neoclassical buildings from its founding in 1749 to the burning of the second church in 1919. In the decades preceding the war that began in 1861, Georgians imitated the fashionable architectural historicisms of New York and Philadelphia. The University of Georgia Chapel at Athens and Savannah's Christ Church, Johnson Square, belong to the succession of Grecian temples that began to dot Southern townscapes in the 1830s. Gothic fantasies like St. John's, Savannah, displayed the influence in Georgia of Richard Upjohn, Frank Wills, and the ecclesiological revival.

But for the most part Georgia churches display only the dilute influence of these pristine historical styles. The beginning of church building in Georgia was dominated by the galleried meetinghouse represented by Jerusalem Church, Rincon (1767) and Midway Church, Liberty County (1792). The eighteenth century saw the flowering of the baroque sermon, in which the preacher manipulated his themes fugue-like. elaborating contrapuntally on a text with layers of example, illustration, and exhortation. The sacraments were received infrequently, but preaching flourished. The convenience of the auditory was everything, and the builders of these galleried churches did for Georgia what Wren had done for London in the 1670s. The long-naved European church had been built to house a sacred spectacle, and was dominated by an axial path that led from sacrament to sacrament, from baptism to the Kingdom of Christ. Preaching brought the hearer to the preacher's feet. The long central aisle, which vacated the best seats, gave way to side aisles. The building was widened and shortened, the gallery added.

Whatever its interior arrangement, the architectural feature of this late-baroque architecture was the system of bays, a certain rhythm of windows and doors as these parade across the elevations. This ubiquitous image inhabits churches built in Georgia from the late eighteenth century to the present, making it hard to distinguish the country architecture of the 1770s from the plain style of the late nineteenth century. The small white building with its neat bays, its belfry, pews, and pulpit, persists as the major pattern of Southern church building. In cities the galleries of Midway Church (now balconies) are still found, and stylish city churches have now returned to a version of the late eighteenth-century classicism that informed the architecture of Georgia's first church buildings. Most local nineteenth-century churches are, except to the most practiced eye, stylistically indeterminate. The clear stylistic themes of eighteenth-century England played themselves out in the borderland that lay between the precise and powerful architectural images of Wren and Gibbs, and the tenuated imagination and circumscribed architectural competency of the Piedmont.

Georgia has always been a borderland, lying between the Appalachians and the Atlantic, between English Carolina and Spanish Florida, between the older colonies of the seaboard and the inland empire that opened before settlers in the nineteenth century. The place was also founded, and to a great degree still exists, in a borderland of ideas, between memories of a coherent organic European order to which political and religious significances were fundamental, and the pluralism and gentle nihilism of modernity. By 1780 the themes of medieval Christianity, to which the great, clear doctrines of the Reformation were proposed as mere amendments, were fading, and the religion of the South, helped along by Awakenings and revivals, was on its way from reality to experience, from religion based on an objective body of revealed truth to that usable preaching that solaces and saves.

Georgia church buildings illuminate this transition. About 1800—somewhat later in the backcountry—the baroque world, a pattern of assertive systems still visible in the facade of Savannah's Independent Presbyterian Church, came to an end, lost in the geographical and intellectual indeterminacy of the American frontier. The Southern colonies were settled at the end of a three-hundred-year development in art and ideas that was itself but a footnote to the civilization of medieval Europe. Wren considered Gothic somewhat rude, and Bellarmine roundly disliked Calvinism, but Wren and the architects of Chartres, Bellarmine, Calvin, and Luther all stand together on the distant side of a great divide that unites the age of reason with the age of faith, and separates both from the age of eclecticism. The architecture that ends in Savannah, Augusta, Charleston, and New Orleans had presumed the existence of reason, form, and precedent. But the age of Jefferson, Paine, and Voltaire was a time not for precedent but for revolution. Americans would quickly exhaust the fading national classicism called Federal, and attention would turn to those experimental engagements with images from the past that would occupy the architectural profession until 1861. The past would lose its place as an unshakable authority and become, under the influence of the newly recognized discipline of history, a storehouse of available images, a mine from which Grecian, Gothic, Elizabethan, castellated, and Italianate images would be quarried at will. When we look at buildings like St. Joseph's, Macon, we are witnessing the search for place and solidity in a dissolving world. We see an architecture pregnant with that modernity to which Sherman's march was midwife. We see Georgians who can understand their lives as extensions of a Grecian ethos, of the *polis* and the Parthenon, or else as actors in the neomedieval scene brought to life by Walter Scott and Augustus Welby Pugin.

As one enjoys the images presented here, it becomes clear that the buildings depicted were never part of a culture that enjoyed religious unity. The Anglican establishment was never successful, and the variety of the churches that succeeded it is an icon of Georgia's religious pluralism. Their names tell their stories: the Catholic necessity and Episcopal custom that the building be named for a saint; the Baptist and Presbyterian preference for numbers and place names; the black tendency, copied from the larger practice of rural Georgians, to name their buildings for the cities visited by Saint Paul or for the sanctuaries of ancient Israel. Style, too, reflects this understanding of religion as a thing of many ways and many histories, from the Gothic and baroque of Roman Catholics to the plain style of the country Methodists and the mock classicism of Greek Revival country churches. Style implies a certain historiography, a certain account of the past. It is not for nothing that Georgia Baptists and Methodists steer clear of Gothic, which offers a positive image of a past they reject, nor is their own preference for the severe Federal, always devoid of images, accidental. In the same way the Romantic Gothicism of nineteenth-century Episcopalians lays claim on a past those worshipers would appropriate. Interiors also tell their story. The Baptists, Presbyterians, and Methodists built preaching houses, places to shelter prayer and preaching. But in churches like Sacred Heart, Augusta, the space is dominated by an altar, above which hangs a crucifix, itself the remainder of a venerable Western iconography. In such a building words are also heard, but actions are also undertaken and things seen.

One of the keys to Georgia culture is the Christ-hauntedness of which Flannery O'Connor wrote. Christ may haunt but never inhabit Southern culture, for a fundamental principle of Southern religion has been and remains the invisibility and spirituality of God, an invisibility that the sternest profession of the Incarnation has not tempered. Many Southerners, and Georgians as much as any, inherit from the Anabaptist influence on the origins of the regional faith a folk Gnosticism that requires that there be no images of Christ, the saints, or the New Jerusalem. Southern religion is a spiritual religion, spiritual in a sense not utterly alien to the Albigensians and Cathari. Images may, indeed must, be musical, and musical with an almost baroque extravagance. The Blood of the Lamb may be praised with song elaborately, but the Lamb Slain who inhabited the European imagination from the Apocalypse to Van Eyck can never be depicted. For images have an objectivity and precision that strains Southern religion. Our regional faith is one in which hearing and feeling inspire private judgment, and in which salvation is not so much belief in the truth as the conclusions of one's soul. The church buildings of Georgia have for the most part sheltered a religion not of truth but of experience, and experience unmoderated is a path not toward the objectivity of worship or involvement with creation but toward the inner light. Truth is one, but experience is various, and the characteristic of Georgia churches that strikes the eye is the pluralism of style that bespeaks a pluralism of religious meanings and foretells the pluralism of twentieth-century American life.

And yet this is not the most important fact to which Georgia churches bear witness. For they are first and most significantly memorials to the belief of a people that God,

in the old-fashioned meaning of the word—not as a consciousness or a force but as Creator and Judge—does exist. To this religious conclusion the church buildings of Georgia bear silent testimony. Liberalism (not generosity or magnanimity, but the belief that no truth capable of binding reason and intellect exists) is the prerogative of persons who believe they can control nature, and hence their own natures and destinies. Life on the land, at least in the nineteenth century, never encouraged that interpretation, and the same lingering inability of ordinary people to believe wholeheartedly the myths of progress and of ultimate technical control keep countless Antiochs and Bethels and Shilohs alive even in an era when satellite dishes point skyward from rural hilltops.

When one looks at the images in this collection, one is viewing the buildings that stood (and often still stand) at the heart of a culture and represent the major influence on Southern civilization. They are often the only building that remains to mark the site of a crossroads town—the school, the post office, and the store having decamped to the county seat. Sometimes the churches are the only buildings in a dozen blocks of urban decay in which flicker any continuity, any hope. They are still, as in colonial Georgia, spiritual centers of every community, purchased through the subscriptions of the congregation, who, now as then, still linger after worship for conversation. In the country the shadows of their steeples and towers fall across the ancestors, and everywhere it is beneath their pulpits that children will marry and begin again the slow rhythm of the generations. Homecoming is a Southern institution whose name expresses the lingering truth that although we may live in Atlanta, or even California, home remains the community in which we last belonged to the land, in which parents and grandparents rest. These ties are stretched; they still remain.

As a building type, churches are the flag of Georgia (and Southern) culture, and when one views these pictures, one sees the body of a culture that lives on beneath the veneer of modernity. Almost none of the buildings in this book is a museum. Each is a form in time and place inspired, in different ways and perhaps even with different wisdoms, by the human engagement with God, and made visible in this book by a painter who has caught the meaning of an important architecture.

James Patrick

A Color Album

Midway Church, Liberty County

Historic Churches and Temples of Georgia

Christ Episcopal Church, St. Simons Island

Congregation Mickve Israel, Savannah

Historic Churches and Temples of Georgia

St. Bartholomew's Episcopal Church, Chatham County

Jerusalem Lutheran Church, Effingham County

Historic Churches and Temples of Georgia

Church of the Most Sacred Heart, Augusta

Mercer Chapel, Penfield

Crescent Hill Baptist Church, Helen

A Color Album

Ebenezer Baptist Church, Atlanta

Historic Churches and Temples of Georgia

Possum Trot Church, Berry College, Mount Berry

St. Joseph's Catholic Church, Macon

Ida Cason Callaway Memorial Chapel, Pine Mountain

Trinity Episcopal Church, Columbus

The Infantry Center Chapel, Ft. Benning

Savannah and the Coast

MIDWAY CHURCH, LIBERTY COUNTY

In 1695 a small group of Puritans from Dorchester, Massachusetts, founded a church-centered community on the Ashley River in South Carolina. Because of overcrowded conditions and worn-out lands, part of the Dorchester Society in turn moved to Midway, Georgia, where, in 1754, they founded the Midway Society, a Congregationalist community in which Christianity and daily living were closely intertwined. The first service was held in the community meeting house in 1758, in the year in which the Anglican Church became the established church of the colony.

The Midway settlers, who colonized the entire parish, played a significant role in early Georgia history. They were people of substantial wealth based on the cultivation of rice, indigo, and other crops. Two of them, Dr. Lyman Hall (a Midway Church member) and Button Gwinnett (an Anglican), along with George Walton of Augusta, were signers of the Declaration of Independence.

The original church was destroyed by the British in 1778. The present church was built in 1792. The Midway Society then prospered until the Civil War, when General William Tecumseh Sherman's army laid waste to the land in 1864. As a result of the devastation of the county, white church members dispersed. For most of the remainder of the nineteenth century Midway Church was a center of black Protestantism. After a period of neglect in the early part of the twentieth century, the church was restored and is once again the site of of regular meetings of the Midway Society.

®On the National Register of Historic Places.

Located in Midway, 30 miles south of Savannah and 29 miles north of Darien on Highway 17.

The Church and Society of Gravel Hill was organized in 1815 as a branch of the Midway Church. At that time, a log building was used for both church and school purposes with Robert Quarterman as the first pastor. In 1836 a frame church was built on land donated by Simon Fraser. The name of both the church and the community were changed to Flemington in 1850 in honor of William Fleming. The present church building was erected in 1852.

The church was served by ministers of the Midway Congregational Church until 1865, when members were no longer able to attend services at Midway. Then they formed a separate organization and adopted the Presbyterian polity. The church became part of the Presbytery of Georgia in 1866.

Perhaps the best-known person interred in the Flemington cemetery is Samuel Dowse Bradwell. After the Civil War he reorganized the Hinesville *Gazette*, served as a state senator and state school commissioner, and was president of the Normal School of Athens, which became a part of the University of Georgia in the 1930s.

®On the National Register of Historic places.

Flemington is nine miles northwest of Midway on Highway 82.

DORCHESTER PRESBYTERIAN CHURCH, LIBERTY COUNTY

The Dorchester Presbyterian Church was built in 1854 on four rural acres in the midst of prosperous rice-growing plantations. Originally, the small congregation used it in the summer months only. In 1871 it was admitted to the Savannah Presbytery.

The church bell is from nearby Sunbury, once a prosperous port city rivaling Savannah. A font and communion service are from Midway Church.

Between Midway and Sunbury; a state historical marker on the roadside marks the Dorchester site.

FIRST PRESBYTERIAN CHURCH, ST. MARYS

In 1808 and 1809 land was donated and public funds were pledged to build what is now the First Presbyterian Church of St. Marys. It was originally nondenominational, but in 1821 a Presbyterian missionary from New Jersey named Horace Pratt arrived and found religion in a "very low and languishing state." He proceeded to organize what became the Independent Presbyterian Church of St. Marys (later First Presbyterian

Church of St. Marys) in 1828 by an act of the Georgia legislature.

The First Presbyterian Church of St. Marys is thought to be the oldest Presbyterian church building in continuous use in Georgia. It is raised clapboard with an open wooden bell tower. The bell in the tower was cast by Paul Revere, one of 389 that he produced. Only a fraction of those are still in use today.

®On the National Register of Historic Places.

Downtown St. Marys—
Osborn Street
at Conyers Street.
St. Marys is on Highway 40,
eight miles east
of I-95 at the Florida border.

ST. MARYS METHODIST CHURCH, ST. MARYS

St. Marys Methodist Church was established in 1799, making it the oldest religious organization in the city. Methodist services were first held in the courthouse. In 1812 the site of the present church was deeded to the Methodists by the city of St. Marys. The first church built there was subsequently given to the Negro Methodists and moved to another site prior to the Civil War. About the same time, the present St. Marys Methodist Church was built. It was occupied by Federal troops in 1862 and was used as a Quartermasters Department, where many animals were butchered.

The church is still active.

®On the National Register of Historic Places.

Downtown St. Marys on Conyers Street.

SARDIS CHURCH, CHARLTON COUNTY

Sardis Church, near Folkston, is the oldest church in Charlton County. The first church edifice was built in this area around 1821 and was subsequently moved to or near its present site in 1840. With twenty-four members, Sardis Church was admitted to the Alapaha River Primitive Baptist Association in 1856.

The church pulpit has been in use for more than one hundred years and bears a bullet scar from the Indian wars. Many of the area's early settlers were buried in the adjacent cemetery.

Georgia Highway 23 about two miles southwest of Folkston.

Historic Churches and Temples of Georgia

CHRIST EPISCOPAL CHURCH, ST. SIMONS ISLAND

The origins of Christ Church date to 1736, when the congregation was established as a mission of the Church of England. The first services were conducted by the Reverend Charles Wesley in the chapel at nearby Fort Frederica. Wesley also preached under the famous Wesley Oak. His first service there in 1736 was attended by General James Oglethorpe, the founder of Georgia. A wooden cross made from the Wesley Oak hangs near the pulpit of the present Christ Episcopal Church.

After the Revolutionary War, the church became part of the newly formed Protestant Episcopal Church. The first church was erected on the property in 1820, three years before it became one of the three parishes organizing the diocese of Georgia. Though saved from near destruction by fire during the Civil War, the original building was eventually torn down and replaced by the present Queen Anne style structure in 1884. It was built under the direction of the Reverend Anson G. P. Dodge, the new minister of Christ Church at that time. Finding the old church in a ruinous condition, he had the present one built on the original foundation.

Within the bucolic setting of the surrounding cemetery are buried a diverse group of people, including Rev. Dodge and his young wife, who died in India. The graves also include those of other former rectors, early settlers, British Army officers, plantation owners and soldiers of every war in which the United States has taken part through the mid-twentieth century.

®Pending nomination on the National Register of Historic Places, 1986.

St. Simons Island, adjacent to Fort Frederica National Park.

LOVELY LANE CHAPEL, EPWORTH-BY-THE-SEA, ST. SIMONS ISLAND

Epworth-By-The-Sea, St. Simons Island.

Lovely Lane Chapel sits on a part of Gasciogne Bluff, which faces Brunswick and at one time guarded the entrance of St. Simons from invaders. The bluff was also the site of a large lumber mill that furnished live oak and heart of pine for furniture, buildings, and ships around the world. One of the ships in which St. Simons wood was used was the U.S.S. *Constitution* ("Old Ironsides") of the War of 1812 fame.

In 1880 the Dodge family built Lovely Lane Chapel (then known as St. James Chapel) as a house of worship for the workers in the lumber mills. It was nondenominational so that all who felt the need could pray there. In 1949 the chapel and surrounding area were taken over by the South Georgia Methodist Conference and renamed Epworth-by-the-Sea, after the boyhood home of John Wesley, who preached for a time on St. Simons Island. Although the chapel is cared for by the Methodists, it remains nondenominational.

Historic Churches and Temples of Georgia

FAITH CHAPEL, JEKYLL ISLAND

Jekyll Island was originally occupied by the Creek Indians, who called it Ospo. It was subsequently occupied by Spanish friars, the British, and, after the Revolutionary War, by a French family. It was during the time of the British occupancy that James Oglethorpe renamed the island for his friend, Sir Joseph Jekyll. In the late 1880s a group of wealthy Northern businessmen searching for a winter resort purchased Jekyll Island. They built private homes, a clubhouse for dining and socializing, and a nondenominational chapel for worship.

Faith Chapel was constructed in 1904. Services were often conducted by well-known bishops, and hymns were sung by a choir made up of clubhouse waiters. Two beautiful stained glass windows adorn the chapel. One is by Helen and M. Armstrong and the other was made and signed by Louis Comfort Tiffany, making it particularly rare and valuable.

When World War II began, the owners of the island left because of the possible danger from enemy warships. They did not return, and the island was sold to the State of Georgia in 1947. The chapel today is well maintained and open to the public.

®On the National Register of Historic Places.

Millionaires' Village, Jekyll Island.

DARIEN PRESBYTERIAN CHURCH, DARIEN

In 1735 the ship *Prince of Wales* sailed from the port of Inverness, Scotland, carrying 130 Highlanders and their minister, the Reverend John McLeod, a native of the Isle of Skye. They had been offered free transportation and free land in the Georgia colony. They settled on the Georgia coast in the town of Darien, named in the memory of the ill-fated Scottish settlement on the Isthmus of Panama. One of their first acts was to build a chapel for divine worship. Located one mile east of the site of the present church, it was the first Presbyterian church established in Georgia.

Since that time, numerous other structures have served the Presbyterians in and around Darien. The second place of worship was a meeting house on the old Savannah Road, eight miles north of Darien, which served all the Presbyterians of St. Andrew's Parish. First Presbyterian Church of Darien was chartered in 1808, when a newer church built near the center of town burned. The first church on the present site, built in 1876, also burned. The present building was erected in 1900.

Downtown Darien
at Third and Jackson Streets.

Historic Churches and Temples of Georgia

SAINT CYPRIAN'S EPISCOPAL CHURCH, DARIEN

Saint Cyprian's Episcopal Church was built in 1876 through the efforts of the Reverend James Wentworth Leigh, Dean of Hereford, England, to serve the needs of "the Colored People of McIntosh County." The church was named after a martyred African bishop. Contributions came from Philadelphia and England as well as the local community.

The church is of "tabby" construction, a common substance in coastal Georgia consisting of a mixture of lime, shells, sand, and water. The church continues to serve a small congregation to the present time.

®On the National Register of Historic Places.

Fort King George Road on the east side of Darien.

CHAPEL OF OUR LADY OF GOOD HOPE, ISLE OF HOPE, CHATHAM COUNTY

The Chapel of Our Lady of Good Hope was established by the Benedictine Fathers in 1874. With this chapel was built the first Benedictine monastery in the South. It is situated in the midst of a rose garden and live oak trees. A block away are many lovely homes facing private docks that open on to one of the many inland waterways in the marshlands of Chatham County. The chapel is still in use for Sunday Mass.

®On the National Register of Historic Places.

Bluff Road and Rosenbrook Avenue, Isle of Hope, off of Skidaway Road in Savannah.

CHRIST EPISCOPAL CHURCH, SAVANNAH

James Oglethorpe, the founder of Georgia, arrived in Savannah on 12 February 1733. Instructed by the trustees of the Anglican Church to select a site for a church building, he chose Johnson Square, the location of the present Christ Episcopal Church.

John Wesley was rector from 1736 to 1737, when he returned to England, discouraged by his stay in the colony. He was replaced by the Reverend George Whitefield, the noted evangelist and founder of Bethesda Orphan Home.

The first church building was completed in 1750 under the direction of the Reverend Bartholomew Zouberbuhler. It contained the first organ in Georgia, donated by Colonel Barnard of Augusta. The church building was destroyed by fire in 1796. The second church building, finished in 1810, was razed in 1838 after it was declared unsafe.

The present building, designed by Georgia architect James Hamilton Couper and built in 1840, is of Greek Revival style and was patterned after the Maison Carre, a Roman Temple in Nimes, France. The interior ceiling was cast from molds designed by Christopher Wren for St. Paul's Cathedral in London.

®On the National Register of Historic Places.

Downtown Savannah at 28 Bull Street.

CONGREGATION MICKVE ISRAEL, SAVANNAH

In January 1733 a group of forty-three Jews sailed from England to Savannah. They came ashore on 11 July, a few months after General James Oglethorpe first landed. Shortly after their arrival, they formed Congregation Mickve Israel in a rented house on Market Square. They brought with them a circumcision box and a Sephar Torah, which the congregation still maintains.

In the 1730s other Jewish colonists arrived. They included both Ashkenazic Jews of German origin and Sephardic Jews of Mediterranean origin. These groups did not cooperate well, so no permanent synagogue was built at that time.

In the late 1730s most Savannah Jews, fearing an inquisition from the Spanish, who had threatened Fort Frederica on St. Simons Island, fled to the safety of South Carolina. They returned to Savannah with many other Jews when the Spanish were defeated.

In 1773 Mordecai Sheftall deeded a tract of land in Savannah for use as a synagogue and cemetery. In 1790 Governor Edward Telfair granted the congregation a perpetual charter. Finally, in 1820, the first synagogue was built at the corner of Whitaker and Perry Lane. It was the first synagogue in Georgia. The present temple, finished in 1878, is located on Monterey Square. The design, unique for a synagogue, is English Gothic.

®On the National Register of Historic Places.

Downtown Savannah on Bull Street (Monterey Square).

ST. JOHN'S EPISCOPAL CHURCH, SAVANNAH

St. John's Episcopal Church is unique in that its character was shaped as much by the adjoining rectory as by the church building itself. Therefore, the two buildings can be described as separate entities.

St. John's Church was organized in 1840 by a committee from Christ Church and was incorporated in 1841. It was first located on the northwest corner of Jones and Whitaker Streets until the present building was completed and consecrated by Bishop Stephen Elliott in 1853. The ten original stained glass windows were fabricated by Moore and Co. of Liverpool, England in 1886. The last two windows were made in 1938 by J. P. Reeves and Co. of Philadelphia in memory of Judge George T. Cann, a longtime vestryman and senior warden.

The rectory is the Green-Meldrim House, built in the early 1850s by Charles Green, a successful English cotton merchant and ship owner. Many of the materials used in its construction came from England as ballast on his ships. The Gothic Revival building was the most elaborate in Savannah at the time. It is best known as the headquarters of General William Tecumseh Sherman after he entered Savannah in December 1864 at the end of his "March to the Sea." While there, he sent his famous telegram to President Lincoln presenting the city of Savannah as a Christmas present.

The house was sold to Judge Peter W. Meldrim in 1892, and in turn to its next door neighbor, St. John's Church in 1943. A walkway was subsequently constructed connecting the two buildings. The kitchens, stable, and servants' quarters of the Green-Meldrim House were converted into the church rectory.

®On the National Register of Historic Places.

Downtown Savannah at One West Macon Street.

Wesley Monumental United Methodist Church was organized in 1868. The actual construction of the church building was begun in 1875 and proceeded in stages over the next fifteen years. The edifice was constructed in the Gothic Revival style and was patterned after Queen's Kirk in Amsterdam, Holland.

The building of the church was greatly aided by many gifts when it became known that it was to be a memorial to John and Charles Wesley. Perhaps the most outstanding features of Wesley Monumental are the stained glass windows, made in the world-famous studio of Louis Comfort Tiffany, who personally supervised their installation.

®On the National Register of Historic Places.

Downtown Savannah at 429 Abercorn.

INDEPENDENT PRESBYTERIAN CHURCH, SAVANNAH

The original Independent Presbyterian Church of Savannah was built on Ellis Square as the result of a 1755 petition to the city council by "Dissenters from the Church of England and Professors of the Doctrine of the Church of Scotland, agreeable to the Westminster Confession of Faith." The first pastor, John Joachim Zubly, spoke to the Provincial Congress of Georgia there.

During the Revolutionary War, the building was used as a magazine by the British and was severely damaged. It burned in 1796 and was rebuilt in 1800 on Telfair Square. This building, too, was extensively damaged, this time by a hurricane. The congregation decided it was too expensive to rebuild, so it built the next structure on Bull Street and Oglethorpe Avenue. It was designed by John Holden Green, the famous Rhode Island architect, and dedicated in 1819 by President James Monroe.

Misfortune continued to plague the church building, which burned in the great fire of 1889, and the present structure was built as a replica of the last one. The marriage of Woodrow Wilson to his first wife, Ellen Axson, was performed in the church's manse by her grandfather, the Reverend I. S. K. Axson.

®On the National Register of Historic Places.

Downtown Savannah at Bull St. and West Oglethorpe.

THE DEVELOPMENT OF BLACK CHURCHES

Prior to the Civil War, most slaves who attended formal worship services did so in white churches, where the seating was segregated. Many slaves also held clandestine religious ceremonies in fields, brush arbors, and in their slave quarters.

Although the proliferation of independent black churches and denominations had to await emancipation, the process actually began much earlier. The first blacks to form their own churches officially did so in the late 1700s, with the founding of the First Bryan and First African Baptist churches of Savannah, soon followed by Springfield Baptist Church in Augusta. The first black denomination, the African Methodist Episcopal (A.M.E.) Church, was founded in Philadelphia in 1816.

Following emancipation, ex-slaves began to build their own communities in earnest. The church was often the first building constructed. Most blacks who were converted to Christianity became Baptists or Methodists, perhaps because the simple process of conversion and open forms of worship allowed for the freest expression of the black religious experience.

Rural black churches were usually simple one-room rectangular frame structures. Interiors were often unplastered and unceiled. Urban churches, although also simple, were generally larger. They were usually built on smaller plots and were less utilized as outdoor social gathering places.

NICHOLSONBORO BAPTIST CHURCH, CHATHAM COUNTY

The original founders of Nicholsonboro Baptist Church were slaves on St. Catherine's Island, owned by a wealthy planter and businessman, Jacob Waldburg. The freedmen stayed there until 1868, when about two hundred of them moved to Cedar Grove, one mile from the site of the present church in Nicholsonville.

The first Nicholsonboro Church was built in the late 1870s on the old White Bluff Road. It is a simple, rectangular frame building. As the congregation grew and prospered, the need for a larger building led to the construction in 1890 of another frame building, the one in current use by the congregation. The older building served as a feasting house until it deteriorated too badly for continued use.

Both churches are significant examples of late nineteenth-century rural black church construction. They are also two of the very few that have survived and perhaps the only two on the same site.

®On the National Register of Historic Places.

White Bluff Road in a section of Chatham County called Nicholsonville on the outskirts of Savannah.

ST. BARTHOLOMEW'S EPISCOPAL CHURCH, CHATHAM COUNTY

St. Bartholomew's Episcopal Church was formed in 1832 to serve Chatham County rice plantation owners and slaves. The church became the educational as well as the religious center for what became the Burroughs community. Before the Civil War slaves were taught basic educational skills there. In 1878 sixteen members of the First Battalion Infantry, Georgia Volunteers, Colored, were sent to the new mission of St. Bartholomew's on the Grove Plantation.

The Women's Auxiliary of St. Bartholomew's Church in New York City sent four hundred dollars to the mission. This donation was used to build a school and chapel. In 1898 the Burroughs community was incorporated into a town in which black residents have served as mayor and council members. It once prospered as a railhead for shipping locally grown vegetables and rice north to Savannah.

The third and present St. Bartholomew's Church was consecrated in 1896. The first was destroyed by a tornado, the second by a hurricane. The church once had more than four hundred members. It subsequently went through a period of neglect, but has been lovingly restored by the local community, mainly through the efforts of Gertrude Green.

®On the National Register of Historic Places.

Located in the Burroughs community in the southwestern corner of Chatham County off US 17 at the end of Chevis Road.

Historic Churches and Temples of Georgia

FIRST AFRICAN BAPTIST *and* FIRST BRYAN BAPTIST CHURCHES, SAVANNAH

The First African Baptist Church of Savannah is the oldest black church in North America. The original congregation consisted of four slaves owned by Jonathan Bryan. They were converted and baptized by the Reverend George Liele, the first black Baptist missionary in America. One of the slaves, Andrew Bryan, began preaching to both blacks and whites in a rough wooden building on Yamacraw Plantation. In 1788 forty-five members were baptized and Andrew Bryan was ordained as the first minister of First African Baptist Church by Abraham Marshall, a white minister from Kiokee.

In 1790 Rev. Bryan bought his freedom, and in 1793 he purchased the lot on which First Bryan Baptist Church now stands. In 1797 the site was sold to the trustees of the First African Baptist Church. In 1832 the congregation divided, and two separate congregations emerged. First African Baptist Church moved to Franklin Square, and First Bryan Baptist Church continued to use the property on Bryan Street purchased in 1793.

First African Baptist Church.
Downtown Savannah at 19 Alfred Street.

First Bryan
Baptist Church.
Downtown Savannah
at 575 West
Bryan Street.

®On the National Register of Historic Places.

ST. PHILIP A.M.E. CHURCH, SAVANNAH

The first African Methodist Episcopal Church in the state of Georgia was organized in Savannah by the Reverend A. L. Stanford in 1865, just after the Civil War ended. It was named St. Philip A.M.E. Church. The church building was completed in the late 1880s, but was demolished during the storm of 1896. The congregation then voted to move the church to a more central location and, therefore, purchased property at West Broad and Charles Streets.

The present brick structure was completed between 1910 and 1915. It has encountered a number of crises, including the collapse of the north wall, a boiler accident leaving the church without heat, and an advertised public sale of the building because of unpaid mortgage debts. But it has survived and at the present time is thriving.

®On the National Register of Historic Places.

Downtown Savannah at 613 West Broad Street.

Jerusalem Lutheran Church is Georgia's oldest surviving religious structure. It is located on the banks of the Savannah River, thirty miles above Savannah. It was constructed of bricks made from clay deposits near the church site, with walls that are twenty-one inches thick. The church, along with its cemetery and one home, are the only remaining original structures of the once thriving town of Ebenezer.

The church was built from 1767 to 1769 by the Salzburgers, a group of exiles from Salzburg, Austria, whose congregation was organized in Augsburg, Germany, in 1733. They first arrived in Savannah in 1734 and founded the town of Ebenezer the same year. They moved to New Ebenezer, the present church site, in 1736. In 1779, when Ebenezer was occupied by the British, the church was used first as a hospital and then as a cavalry horse stable. The town was liberated in 1782 by forces led by General Anthony Wayne. That same year, the Georgia legislature met in the church.

®On the National Register of Historic Places.

Located in Springfield, 30 miles north of Savannah off Highway 21, in Effingham County.

GOSHEN CHURCH, EFFINGHAM COUNTY

The first Moravians in North America came to Georgia in 1735. Their commitments to pacifism, religious freedom, and missions to Indians and slaves led to conflict with the surrounding community. Many of the Moravians moved to Pennsylvania, and by 1740 no Moravians were left in Georgia.

Then, in 1774 an undersecretary of state in London asked for missionaries to preach the gospel to the slaves on his Georgia plantation at Knoxborough. Two Moravian missionaries sent there began to preach in a little place nearby named Goshen, in a church that had been built by subscription from Germans and Englishmen living in the neighborhood, and had been used regularly by the Salzburger Lutherans from Ebenezer as an outlying church, served by the Jerusa-lem Church clergy. In 1775 one of the Moravian missionaries died from the "fever," which was always prevalent on the local rice plantations in the summertime. The other missionary stayed until 1779 and then returned to England. In 1820 the Methodists began using the Goshen church building, which was eventually deeded to the Methodist Conference.

Located on Highway 21 north of Savannah, near Springfield.

Augusta and Northeast Georgia

ST. PAUL'S CHURCH, AUGUSTA

The land on which St. Paul's Church is located is perhaps the most historic site in Augusta. It was initially selected by fur traders Kennedy O'Brien and Roger Lacy as a site for an Indian trading post. In 1736 the Georgia Trustees authorized the construction of a fort on the site. It was to be called Fort Augusta after a British royal princess. In 1750 the first St. Paul's Church was built "under the curtain of the Fort."

In 1763 the chiefs of the major regional Indian tribes met at Fort Augusta with the governors of Georgia, North and South Carolina, and Virginia, as well as the king's representative to sign a historic treaty. Ten years later, in another meeting at Fort Augusta, the Creeks and Cherokees ceded two million acres of North Georgia territory to the British.

During the Revolutionary War, the British erected Fort Cornwallis on the site. It was the focus of several battles and was permanently removed in 1786, to be replaced by a nondenominational church built by the Richmond Academy. In 1818 the Episcopalians were given the site, on which they constructed a second St. Paul's Church. It was destroyed by fire in 1916 and replaced by the present structure.

Among those buried in the surrounding church cemetery is Colonel William Few, Jr., senator, civic leader, and one of two Georgia signers of the U. S. Constitution.

®On the National Register of Historic Places.

Downtown Augusta at 605 Reynolds Street.

SPRINGFIELD BAPTIST CHURCH, AUGUSTA

The original Springfield Baptist Church building was constructed in 1801 for St. John's Methodist Church. In 1844 it was sold to the Springfield Baptist Church congregation and moved to its present location to make room for a new Methodist church.

Springfield Baptist Church was actually founded about 1790 by members of one of the earliest black Baptist churches in America at Silver Bluff, South Carolina. The con-gregation along with its pastors had fled Silver Bluff to Augusta in 1778 to escape British occupation.

The present Springfield Baptist Church edifice was erected in 1897 with a small grave-yard in front for former pastors. The interior has been meticulously restored and the congregation still meets regularly. The original church building still stands behind the present one.

®On the National Register of Historic Places.

Downtown Augusta at 114 12th Street.

FIRST PRESBYTERIAN CHURCH, AUGUSTA

The First Presbyterian Church of Augusta was organized in 1804 by the Reverend Washington McNight, the rector of Richmond Academy. The congregation first met at the site of St. Paul's Episcopal Church, but was soon given a lot on the Richmond Academy grounds. The cornerstone of the present church was laid in 1809, and the building was completed in 1812. In 1881 the Sunday School was added, and the church building was renovated in 1892.

In 1861 the General Assembly of the Presbyterian Church in the United States was organized here. Soon afterwards the church and grounds were used for a hospital and prisoner-of-war camp for Civil War soldiers. From 1858 to 1870 the pastor was the Reverend Joseph R. Wilson, father of President Woodrow Wilson, who lived across the street from the church during his boyhood years.

®On the National Register of Historic Places.

Downtown Augusta at 642 Telfair.

CHURCH OF THE MOST SACRED HEART, AUGUSTA

The first Church of the Most Sacred Heart, along with Sacred Heart Hall, was built in 1874 to accommodate the growing number of Irish Catholics who had originally come to Augusta to escape the potato famine and to work on the Augusta canal and the railroad from Hamburg to Charleston. The present edifice was begun in 1890, when the membership had outgrown the original building. Because it is so ornate, the construction was not completed until 1900.

The architectural style is Romanesque and Gothic, with no less than fourteen patterns of brickwork. A special diamond-shaped brick was inlaid and interlocked with triangular and rectangular bricks to produce the final effect. The brick contractor was so pleased with his work that he remained in Augusta and opened his own brick and tile company.

The Church of the Most Sacred Heart served the Catholic community of Augusta until 1971, when the last mass was said there. It then lay unused for a number of years until it was purchased by the Knoxes, a family active in historic preservation in downtown Augusta. It is presently being used as an art center, and plans are under way for a major restoration of this unique structure.

®On the National Register of Historic Places.

Downtown Augusta at 1306 Ellis Street.

Historic Churches and Temples of Georgia

KIOKEE BAPTIST CHURCH, APPLING

Kiokee Church is not only the first regularly constituted Baptist congregation in Georgia, but is also the oldest one in continuous existence. It was organized in 1772 by the Reverend Daniel Marshall, one of the founders of the Baptist faith in Georgia.

After a meeting house was erected at Kiokee, Marshall ministered to an ever increasing number of Baptists in the area. Sometime after his death in 1784, the church was moved to Appling and a new brick structure was erected.

®On the National Register of Historic Places.

Appling is in Columbia County on Highway 17.

THE MASONIC TEMPLE, WASHINGTON

The Masonic Temple in Washington, though not a house of worship, is closely associated historically with religion. In fact, it actually began as Washington's second Methodist church building in 1881. The initial Methodist church, on the same site, built in 1821, was also Washington's first church of any denomination.

When the Methodists erected their third church building on a different site, they sold this structure to the Masons. Since the Temple has no second story, the Masons had to receive special dispensation to meet on the ground floor.

Downtown Washington on Liberty Street.

WASHINGTON PRESBYTERIAN CHURCH, WASHINGTON

Washington Presbyterian Church was organized in 1790 by the Reverend John Springer, the first ordained Presbyterian minister in the state of Georgia. The congregation met in many places until the present church was built in 1825 on land donated by Dr. Joel Abbott. Dr. Abbott also built the nearby frame house that later became the home of Robert Toombs, United States senator and secretary of state of the Confederacy. In 1821 the South Carolina and Georgia Synod met in Washington to organize the Georgia Presbytery. It met again in Washington in 1826, this time in the church building.

The first pastor of Washington Presbyterian Church, Alexander Hamilton Webster, is buried between the two front doors. Subsequent pastors included Joseph R. Wilson, father of Woodrow Wilson, and Rev. I. S. K. Axson and Dr. Mathew Hoyt, the two grandfathers of Ellen Axson, Woodrow Wilson's first wife. Other famous names associated with the church are lifelong members Alexander H. Stephens, vice-president of the Confederacy, and Duncan G. Campbell, who drafted the treaty removing the Cherokee Indians from Georgia and who introduced the first bill in the Georgia legislature providing for higher education for women.

The church building itself is patterned after a New England colonial church. The sanctuary has remained virtually unchanged; only a vestibule and a Sunday School annex have been added.

®On the National Register of Historic Places.

Downtown Washington at 206 East Robert Toombs Avenue.

LINCOLNTON PRESBYTERIAN CHURCH, LINCOLNTON

Lincolnton Presbyterian Church was established in 1823 when Colonel Peter Lamar, a Presbyterian, donated a three-acre tract of land for religious schooling purposes. The church was built shortly afterwards and was originally used by Methodists, Baptists, and Presbyterians alike. Since the early twentieth century, it has been used exclusively by Presbyterians.

Lincolnton Presbyterian Church is a mission church under the jurisdiction of the Home Mission Committee of the Augusta Presbytery. It has never had a large, self-sustaining congregation. At the present time, the minister for the Washington Presbyterian Church conducts services in Lincolnton.

®On the National Register of Historic Places.

Downtown Lincolnton,
Lincoln County.

LIBERTY CHAPEL, GREENE COUNTY

Liberty Chapel, the "Cradle of Methodism" for Greene and surrounding counties, had its beginnings around 1786 as a brush arbor, which was used as a center for camp meetings. The Reverend James Jenkins reported in 1797 that after a "fiery exhortation" a man in uniform came down the aisle and fell to his knees asking for pardon. Thus, it is claimed, at Liberty Chapel began the Methodist custom of "going to the altar."

Over the years, many famous Methodists, such as Bishop Francis Asbury, have preached at Liberty Chapel.

Greene County, south of I-20.

MERCER CHAPEL, PENFIELD

Mercer Institute, later known as Mercer University, was founded in 1833 on acreage in Greene County donated by Josiah Penfield. In addition to an academy building, a chapel was erected in 1846. In 1871 the Mercer trustees moved the institution to Macon. In 1880 all the holdings in Penfield were given to the Georgia Baptist Association, except for the Penfield cemetery, where Jesse Mercer himself as well as other notable early Mercerians are interred.

The academy building, which has since burned, became the Penfield public school building. The Penfield Chapel was given to the Penfield Baptist Church. In 1949 it was restored and is still in active service.

®On the National Register of Historic Places.

Located seven miles due north of Greensboro in Greene County.

BETHESDA BAPTIST CHURCH, GREENE COUNTY

Bethesda Baptist Church was organized in 1785, at which time it was known as Whatley's Mill Church. The name was changed to Bethesda Baptist Church in 1818, when the present brick structure was erected. Although the surrounding area at that time was well populated and prosperous, the early worshipers, fearful of attack by Indians, often carried their guns to services. Jesse Mercer served as pastor for a number of years.

Located in Greene County about one mile off Highway 44 near Union Point.

Downtown Madison at 383 South Main.

Madison Presbyterian Church was built in 1842 on an old English design. Presbyterians, however, have been active in Morgan County since its inception in 1807. Ellen Axson, Woodrow Wilson's first wife, worshiped here when her father served as pastor in 1866

During the Civil War, the communion service was taken from the church by Union troops who occupied Madison during Sherman's March to the Sea. Later, the general in charge of the occupying force ordered it to be returned. The communion service is on display at the Madison-Morgan Cultural Center.

®On the National Register of Historic Places.

BETHLEHEM BAPTIST CHURCH, MADISON

Bethlehem Baptist Church is a late nineteenth-century rural black church with a
number of features typical of the period,
including a simple wooden frame construction, gabled roof without ornamentation,
and centered entrance. The towers might
have been added later. There is a graveyard
in the woods nearby.

*Located south of Madison
on Pierce Dairy Road off
Highway 441 near I-20.*

FIRST AFRICAN METHODIST EPISCOPAL CHURCH, ATHENS

The precursor of the First A.M.E. Church of Athens was organized in 1866 as a result of the efforts of Henry McNeal Turner, the first black army chaplain, who helped establish many A.M.E. churches in Georgia. The church in Athens is known as Pierce's Chapel, after the Reverend Lovick Pierce, a white leader in Southern Methodism. Pierce's Chapel, on the banks of the Oconee River, had a school for children and adults in the basement. This school proved to be the forerunner of the Athens public school system.

The present lot was purchased in 1881 and the church building itself was constructed in 1916. It is of the medieval style with many eclectic features, showing the relative prosperity of the black community of Athens, which it continues to serve to this day.

®On the National Register of Historic Places.

Downtown Athens at 521 North Hull Street.

UNIVERSITY CHAPEL, ATHENS

The University of Georgia, chartered in 1785, is the oldest chartered state university in the United States. The institution actually began classes in 1801 on a tract of land given by then Governor John Milledge. The first chapel, a wooden one, was replaced in 1832 by the present simple, Doric-columned, brick-and-cement-covered structure.

During the Civil War, the university was closed. Shortly afterwards, Union soldiers occupied the campus and badly damaged the chapel, allegedly burning wooden pews for firewood and using the columns for target practice. In 1867 the university received

a huge painting by the Virginia artist George Cook depicting the interior of St. Peter's Cathedral in Rome. It takes up the entire rear wall of the chapel and is considered one of the most outstanding paintings in America.

In addition to worship services, graduation exercises were held for many years in the chapel. Orations by such famous men as Robert Toombs, Alexander Stephens, and Henry Grady were delivered there over the years. Although the chapel no longer has regularly scheduled services or graduation exercises, it is still used for numerous functions, such as faculty meetings and musical

programs. Also, the bell is traditionally rung by freshmen until midnight following a University of Georgia football victory.

®On the National Register of Historic Places.

Broad Street at College Avenue in Athens.

SENEY-STOVALL CHAPEL, ATHENS

The Seney-Stovall Chapel was built at the Lucy Cobb Institute in 1882 as a gift from George I. Seney, New York philanthropist. His contribution, which was more than matched by the city of Athens, was motivated by a letter written by an Athens girl, Nellie Stovall. The structure, designed by architect W. W. Thomas, is in the shape of a double-linked octagon. An ornate Victorian porch adorns the front.

The chapel housed religious services of all kinds for girls attending the Lucy Cobb Institute, which was founded before the Civil War. The chapel was also used for graduation exercises, recitals, lectures, plays, pageants, and other community events. The school and chapel were abandoned during the Great Depression, at a time when the University of Georgia also began accepting women students. The chapel fell into disrepair, but is presently being restored with a grant from the federal government.

®On the National Register of Historic Places.

Located at Lucy Cobb Institute on Milledge Avenue in Athens.

ASHFORD MEMORIAL METHODIST CHURCH, WATKINSVILLE

Ashford Memorial Methodist Church was built in 1893 in memory of Louisa Booth Ashford by her brothers and children, and was deeded to the Methodist Church the following year. The Victorian architecture is Queen Anne style with Stick and Eastlake variations, so appropriate for smaller churches.

The building was operated by the United Methodists until 1983, when it was abandoned and later sold to an independent Methodist congregation. Among the present members are descendants of the original Ashford family that constructed the church.

Located on Highway 441 in Watkinsville, eight miles south of Athens.

NACOOCHEE PRESBYTERIAN CHURCH, SAUTEE

Nacoochee Presbyterian Church was organized in 1860 by Captain J. H. Nichols, a prominent land owner in present-day Helen, who had a church built on his property in the Nacoochee valley. The valley had belonged to the Cherokee Indians until 1819, when it was ceded to the U.S. Government. It was there at Duke's Creek that gold was first discovered in Georgia.

Capt. Nichols's church served the Presbyterians of the valley until 1898, when it was dissolved by the Athens Presbytery. Later

the presbytery sold the building to the Baptists, who renamed it Crescent Hill Baptist Church. The transfer to the Baptists occurred about the time that the Hardeman family bought the entire Nichols property. Since Mr. Hardeman was a staunch Baptist, he was responsible for the conversion of the building to that denomination, making Crescent Hill Baptist Church one of the few high Victorian style Baptist churches in the state of Georgia. According to Mr. Hardeman's will, the church must remain Baptist

Located off Highway 17 near Sautee store, between Helen and Clarkesville.

Historic Churches and Temples of Georgia

or revert to his descendants, who still own the property.

The Presbyterians, meanwhile, were transferred to the Clarkesville Presbyterian Church. They then worshiped at the Na- coochee Institute Auditorium from 1903 to 1926, when it burned. The present building in Sautee was completed in 1927, and the congregation has prospered there ever since.

®On the National Register of Historic Places.

Located two miles south of Helen on Highway 17.

GRACE PROTESTANT EPISCOPAL CHURCH, CLARKESVILLE

Downtown Clarkesville off Highway 441, Habersham County.

The first Episcopal service in Clarkesville was held in 1838 by the Reverend Ezra B. Kellogg, a missionary sent from New York to the Diocese of Georgia. At his home that same year, Grace Church was organized for three local Episcopalian families and for the many coastal families of that denomination who spent their summers in Clarkesville to escape the humidity.

In 1839 Grace Church was admitted to the diocese and work was begun on the present church building. Until it was completed in 1842, services were held in the Methodist church and at Clarkesville Academy. Prominent early members included Richard W. Habersham, Sr. and Jr., and George R. Jessup.

®On the National Register of Historic Places.

Atlanta and Northwest Georgia

"In 1847 Atlanta was still a shantytown of 2500 inhabitants, 30 stores and 2 hotels, surrounded by woods. The streets were filled with stumps but alive with people in progress. There were no churches and preaching was held, prophetically, in the railroad depot."

Mills Lane, *The People of Georgia*

SHRINE OF THE IMMACULATE CONCEPTION, ATLANTA

®On the National Register of Historic Places.

The city of Atlanta had its rudimentary beginnings in 1837 as the terminus for the Western and Atlantic Railroad. Soon a merchant class arrived to take advantage of this circumstance and to make Atlanta grow. Among them were many Catholics, mostly of Irish descent. The Atlanta Catholic congregation began in 1846; the first church, a frame building on the same site as the present one, was erected in 1848. During the 1850s Georgia prospered as the "Empire State of the South" and many more Catholics continued to arrive until the time of the Civil War.

During the war Atlanta was a major hospital site for wounded soldiers of both sides. The main activity of the congregation was to minister to them. Federal troops under General William Tecumseh Sherman (whose son later became a Jesuit priest) captured the city in 1864, but the church was left virtually intact. Nevertheless, the building was becoming too small, so it was later moved to an adjacent lot and the present church was constructed from 1869 to 1872. Father James O'Brien, the pastor, donated the property of St. Joseph's Infirmary, Atlanta's first permanent hospital, during the 1880 dedication of the marble high altar.

As Atlanta grew, new parishes were started in the suburbs. This fact, coupled with the Great Depression of the 1930s and the general exodus of residences from the downtown area, contributed to the dramatic decline of membership in Immaculate Conception parish. But renewed efforts in the 1950s helped to restore viability to the church.

Then in 1982 the Shrine, which had been saved from the ravages of Union soldiers, burned, leaving only a shell. Practically the only remaining artifacts were two crypts in the basement. One contains the remains of Father Thomas O'Reilly, pastor of the Shrine of the Immaculate Conception when Sherman captured Atlanta. He is credited with saving five churches, including his own, as well as the City Hall, the courthouse, and a number of private residences during the burning of Atlanta. Rebuilding of the church was begun almost immediately after it was burned, and it was rededicated in 1984.

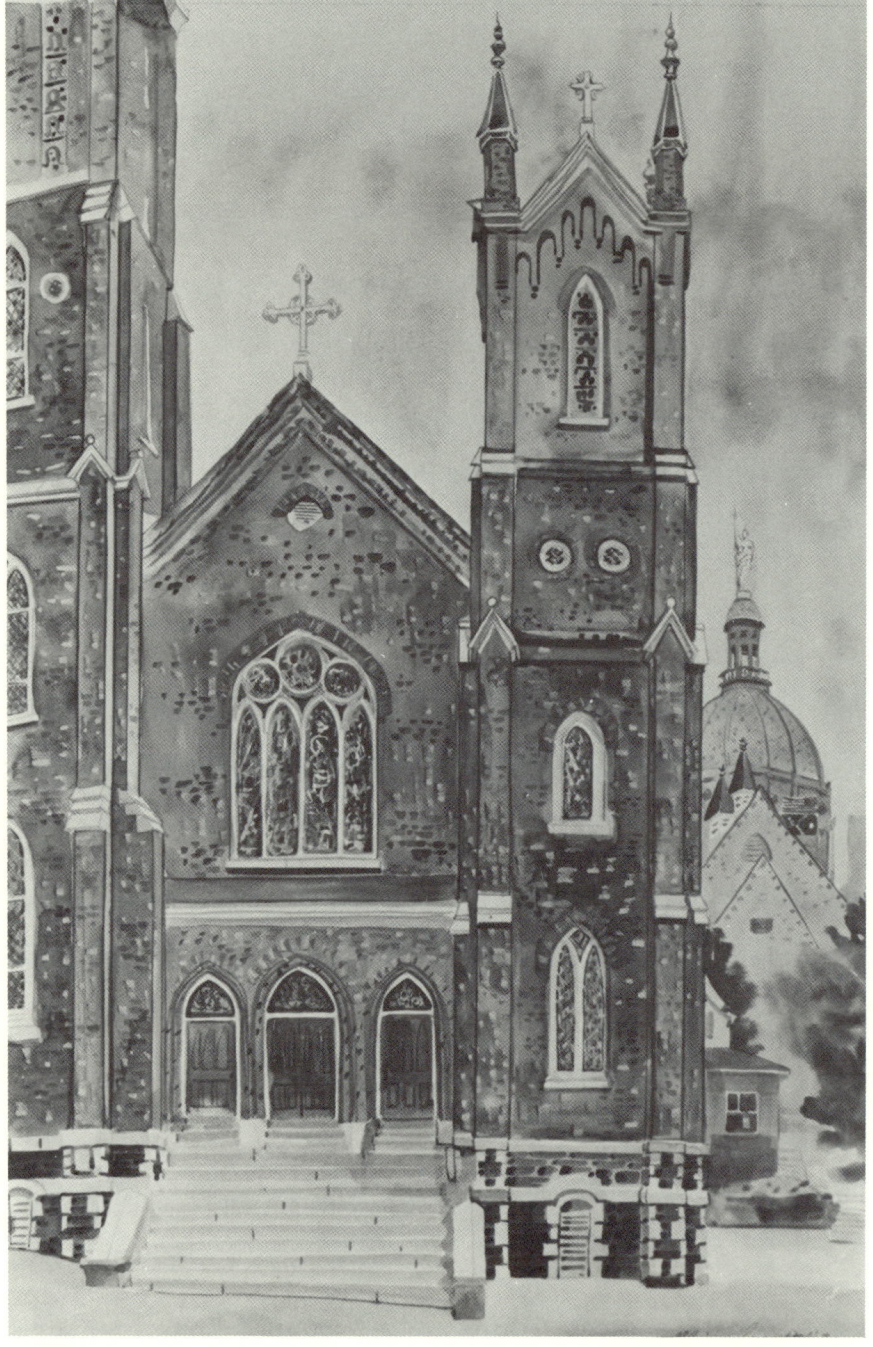

Downtown Atlanta at 48 Martin Luther King Drive Southwest.

CHURCH OF THE SACRED HEART OF JESUS, ATLANTA

The Church of the Sacred Heart of Jesus was designed by well-known Atlanta architect W. T. Downing. He was commissioned by the Marist Fathers to build a French-Romanesque structure. Particularly noteworthy features of the church are the stained-glass windows and the nave. Made in Munich, the windows followed the traditions of medieval cathedrals, teaching the congregation the history of salvation through pictures. The stained-glass windows of Sacred Heart Church tell the story of the life of Christ.

The congregation, which had worshiped in a small frame house on Marietta Street, moved into the present church in 1897. At that time, many thought the building was too far out of town to sustain its membership. But it has continued to function to this day as Atlanta has grown far beyond it.

®On the National Register of Historic Places.

Downtown Atlanta at 353 Peachtree Street Northeast.

North Avenue Presbyterian Church was organized in 1898, with charter members from other Presbyterian churches in Atlanta and Athens. The church building, formally opened in 1901, stands like a medieval fortress on the busy downtown corner of Peachtree Street and North Avenue. It is made of granite from nearby Stone Mountain.

Today, the church has more than one thousand members and serves many more in the community.

®On the National Register of Historic Places.

Downtown Atlanta at 607 Peachtree Street.

FIRST CONGREGATIONAL CHURCH, ATLANTA

The First Congregational Church of Atlanta grew out of a mission established in 1867 by the Reverend and Mrs. Frederick Ayer of Wisconsin in connection with the Storr's School. The school was a pioneer institution for the education of black freedmen and their children. The first place of worship was the chapel of the school; the second, a "little red church." Of the ten original members of the church, seven were black and three were white.

Under the guidance of Dr. Henry U. Proctor, starting in 1894, the church prospered and rapidly increased its membership. It became the largest black Congregational church in the nation, introducing social welfare services unusual in Southern churches.

Dr. Proctor's work culminated in 1908 with the erection of the present church edifice. The Renaissance Revival church has long been known as a meeting ground for community leaders, both black and white. Among the present members is Andrew Young, the mayor of Atlanta.

A rose window in the rear of the church is dedicated to Edmund Asa Ware, founder of Atlanta University, who came to Georgia to set up an educational center for freed slaves after President Abraham Lincoln signed the Emancipation Proclamation.

®On the National Register of Historic Places.

Downtown Atlanta at 105 Courtland.

BUTLER STREET CHRISTIAN METHODIST EPISCOPAL CHURCH, ATLANTA

Butler Street C.M.E. Church grew from a denomination that broke away from the Methodist Episcopal Church, South, in 1870. C.M.E. originally stood for Colored Methodist Episcopal, but the Butler Street Church name was later changed to Christian Methodist Episcopal so as not to give the impression that the church accepted black members only.

The church was organized by the Reverend S. E. Poe in 1882 from a Sunday School on Gilmer Street. The first church was a wooden frame structure. The present one, built in 1920, is of Neo-Gothic Revival style. It was constructed on land donated by Atlanta developer John T. Grant in honor of his former slaves and was dedicated to Bishop Lucious H. Holsey, who was promi-

nent in establishing many C.M.E. churches in Georgia.

The C.M.E. Church on Butler Street attempts to address the wants of the poor in the downtown Atlanta area by feeding the needy six days a week through the Open Door Community program.

®On the National Register of Historic Places.

Downtown Atlanta at 23 Butler Street.

Historic Churches and Temples of Georgia

EBENEZER BAPTIST CHURCH, ATLANTA

Ebenezer Baptist Church was founded in 1886. The present structure on Auburn Avenue was completed in 1922. From 1914 to 1922 the congregation worshiped in the basement while the structure was being completed. In 1931 the Reverend Martin Luther King, Sr., became only the third pastor of Ebenezer Baptist Church. During his long tenure, which ended in 1975, numerous improvements both to the church and to the surrounding community were accomplished.

Rev. King was joined in 1960 by his son, Dr. Martin Luther King, Jr., as copastor. Dr. King, Jr., also brought many changes to the church, including affiliation with the Progressive National Baptist and American Baptist Conventions. During this time he gained an international reputation as an advocate of nonviolent social change. Since the assassination of Dr. King, Jr., in 1968, Ebenezer Baptist Church has often been called "the only religious shrine in America."

®On the National Register of Historic Places.

Downtown Atlanta at Auburn Avenue and Jackson Street Northeast.

THE TEMPLE, ATLANTA

The Temple on Peachtree Street is the third home of the Hebrew Benevolent Society, Atlanta's oldest Jewish congregation, which was founded in 1860 to serve the religious needs of a growing number of German-Jewish immigrants. The first synagogue was built in downtown Atlanta in 1875, the second in 1902.

The present structure, completed in 1931, was designed by a nationally famous Atlanta architect, Philip T. Shutze. It is Neo-Classic in style, best known for its rich interior, particularly its intricate plaster relief work.

The Temple's congregation has been known from its inception for its work in the community. The English-German-Hebrew Academy, founded in 1869, was a forerunner of the Atlanta public school system. The Council of Jewish Women campaigned actively for the abolition of child labor and for the eight-hour work day.

Starting in the early 1900s, Rabbi David Marx began an interfaith Thanksgiving service which became a tradition at The Temple.

Under the leadership of Rabbi Jacob Rothschild, the active involvement of the congregation in the civil rights movement resulted in the bombing of The Temple in 1958. It has since been rebuilt to its former beauty and continues to serve a large segment of Atlanta's Jewish community.

Downtown Atlanta at 1589 Peachtree Street Northwest.

®On the National Register of Historic Places.

PEACHTREE CHRISTIAN CHURCH, ATLANTA

Construction of Peachtree Christian Church was begun on Mother's Day, 1925, and was completed in 1928. Its principal donor was Mr. A. G. Rhodes, a church member, who also donated the land for the church. Mr. Rhodes, whose son-in-law, Rev. L. O. Bricker, was the founding minister, unfortunately did not live to see the building completed.

The building itself is a replica of the fifteenth-century Gothic style Melrose Abbey, a church outside London that was destroyed during a German bombing raid in World War II. The later structure differed from its English progenitor by using local materials, such as brick, rather than stone that was predominant in medieval times. The church was designed by Charles H. Hopson of Atlanta, an English-born architect and church member, who was best known for his ecclesiastical structures. The edifice contains a large collection of stained glass windows, handmade by the London firm of William Glasby.

The Christian church is one of Georgia's smaller religious communities but one of its most open. At the 1928 dedication of Peachtree Christian Church, its leaders announced that the church was a "House of Prayer" for all people and that "no unkind word will ever be said of anybody's race or religion."

®On the National Register of Historic Places.

Downtown Atlanta at 1580 Peachtree Street Northwest.

MOUNT GILEAD METHODIST CHURCH, FULTON COUNTY

Mount Gilead Methodist Church was founded in 1824 by the Reverend John M. Smith, who is buried in the nearby cemetery. As one of the first churches in Fulton County, it claimed many of the county's early settlers as members.

During the Civil War the church was used as a hospital for Confederate and Union soldiers alike. The area was also the site of a skirmish during the Battle of Atlanta. The church itself has been rebuilt several times.

Bolton-Fairburn Road,
1.7 miles south of
Ben Hill in
Fulton County.

54   *Historic Churches and Temples of Georgia*

METHODIST EPISCOPAL CHURCH, OXFORD

The Methodist Episcopal Church of Oxford was built in 1841 under the direction of William Capers, a prominent nineteenth-century Methodist Episcopal bishop. Since that time, additions have been made, including a stage and two wings in 1878, giving the church the appearance of a "rambling house," as Bishop Candler called it. The building, which has not been used for regular worship for more than fifty years, is presently being restored.

Oxford Methodist Episcopal Church has been the scene of two especially noteworthy events. The first concerned a female slave. Bishop James O. Andrew inherited a slave named Kitty Andrew Shell, who worshiped in the church. By church policy, he could not own a slave; by state law, he could not set her free. This impasse was the impetus for the 1845 split between the Methodist churches, North and South.

The other incident of note was the "New South" sermon preached by Bishop Atticus Haygood in 1880. As a result of its national publication, George Sweeny, a prominent New York railroad man, donated $130,000 for education in the South. The money went to Emory College for construction of the main building on the Emory-Oxford campus.

On Wesley Street at Fletcher Street; Oxford is on I-20, 35 miles east of Atlanta.

®On the National Register of Historic Places.

ROSWELL PRESBYTERIAN CHURCH, ROSWELL

Roswell Presbyterian Church was organized in 1839 by the Reverend Nathaniel A. Pratt of Darien, where the earliest Presbyterians had located in Georgia. The early rolls contain many illustrious names. Barrington King, landowner and brother of Roswell King, for whom the town was named, was an original elder in the church. The Bullochs, a prominent Roswell family, claimed as one of its members the mother of President Theodore Roosevelt. Several members, including slaves, became missionaries to South America or Africa.

In 1864 a Union cavalry corps took over the church for a hospital. They removed the furnishings, which were returned intact except for the pipe organ. During the occupation the silver communion service, still in use today, was hidden in a barrel at the home of one of the church members.

®On the National Register of Historic Places.

Mimosa Boulevard in Roswell—20 miles north of Atlanta.

Historic Churches and Temples of Georgia

SAM JONES MEMORIAL FIRST UNITED METHODIST CHURCH, CARTERSVILLE

The First Methodist Church near Cartersville was built around 1838 of log construction, and was located on the Cassville Mission. Soon after, south of Cassville near the Etowah River, Cartersville was founded on the railroad line. As Cartersville grew, the congregation in Cassville decided to move there, and built a second (wooden) church, which was also the first church building in Cartersville.

In 1872 a third and larger brick church was built on the same site, but it too proved to be too small, so in 1907 the present structure was completed. During its construction the famous Methodist evangelist and Cartersville resident, Sam P. Jones, died. The congregation decided to name the church after him in gratitude for his services.

Sam Jones was nationally renowned for his inspiring religious speeches throughout the country. He also held interfaith revivals from 1886 to 1906 in Cartersville in an open-air structure known as "The Tabernacle." Thousands attended this annual September event.

®On the National Register of Historic Places.

Downtown Cartersville.

PINE LOG METHODIST CHURCH, PINE LOG

The town of Pine Log near Cartersville was settled by white people in the early 1830s. It got its name from the Cherokee word for pine tree—"natchez." Pine Log Church was organized in 1834 by Stephen Ellis, one of the early settlers. The present frame church building was erected in 1842. Church membership grew as the population prospered until the Civil War, which resulted in economic stagnation in Pine Log, as in many other communities in the South. Since then, Pine Log and Pine Log Methodist Church populations have remained small.

Pine Log Church is perhaps best known for its camp meetings, held in an arbor and in open sheds near the church and adjoining cemetery. People have come for extensive prayer meetings and have stayed in wooden "tents" (buildings) nearby. The first post-Civil War annual meeting in 1886 was also the most famous. It was then that the evangelist J. N. Sullivan was delivering a sermon, which was not being received enthusiastically, so he asked for divine aid by saying "if it takes it . . . shake the ground on which this old building stands." Almost immediately, shaking did indeed begin, inspiring an intense emotional outpouring. The next day the worshipers discovered they had felt the earthquake that had devastated much of Charleston. The camp meetings have continued each year since then.

Roadway 140, one-quarter mile west of Highway 411 in Bartow County.

®On the National Register of Historic Places.

FIRST UNITED METHODIST CHURCH, ROME

The history of the Methodist Church in Rome actually predates the founding of the city by nine years. In 1825 John B. McFerrin was sent from Nashville as a Methodist minister to organize the First Methodist Church of Rome. The first building was a wooden structure, which was replaced by a brick one in 1852.

The present lot was purchased in 1880, and the current ornate church was constructed from 1884 to 1888. It is Gothic Romanesque in design and built of handmade pinkish bricks. The stained glass windows are thought to be from Austria. A new addition was built in 1965 to accommodate the growing membership.

®On the National Register of Historic Places.

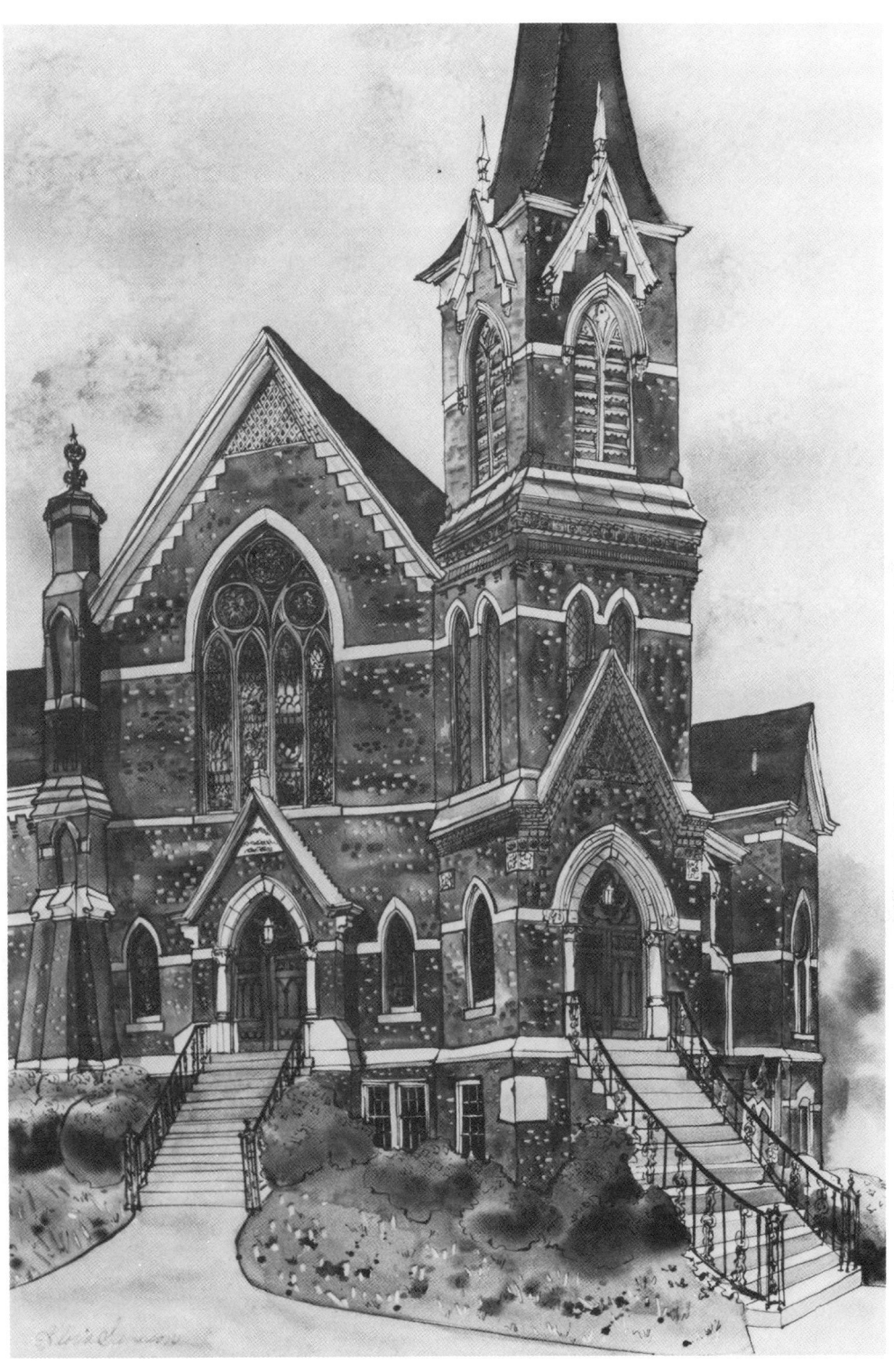

Downtown Rome at 202 East Third Avenue.

POSSUM TROT CHURCH, BERRY COLLEGE, MOUNT BERRY

Possum Trot Church was built between 1850 and 1860. It was attended by Martha Berry as a child. She also visited people in the back hill country of Possum Trot with her father, taking food and clothing to the needy. In 1900 she took over Possum Trot Church and started Possum Trot Sunday School to further attend to the needs of the hill people. Adjoining the church, a day school was later added; it functioned until closing in 1954. Miss Berry, known as "the Sunday Lady of Possum Trot," painted Scriptures on the church walls to make up for a lack of Bibles. Some of the sayings still remain.

The church, which is being restored by Berry College students, is the scene of Possum Trot Homecoming each September, with "dinner on the grounds" between "preaching" and "singing."

®On the National Register of Historic Places.

Berry College Campus, US Highway 27 adjoining Rome.

JERUSALEM BAPTIST CHURCH, PICKENS COUNTY

Jerusalem Baptist Church was built in 1858 in a rural section of Pickens County near Jasper, a small community in the heart of the marble-producing area of the North Georgia mountains. The land was given by Elishe Bennett and Alfred Smith to John Roper, the trustee and deacon of the church. More land was given in 1869 by Solomon C. Palmer for a cemetery.

Southwest of Jasper, Pickens County.

OLD STONE CHURCH, RINGGOLD

The Old Stone Church, organized in 1837, was the first church in Catoosa County. It was organized by a group of Scotch-Irish settlers from the Carolinas and Tennessee. The building itself was constructed in 1850 of local sandstone. Following the Battle of Ringgold in 1863, prior to the Union advance to Atlanta, the church was used as a hospital.

The church was Presbyterian until 1920, when it was bought by a Methodist congregation. It later passed into private hands, but was subsequently repurchased by descendants of the original worshipers to be used by various denominations.

®On the National Register of Historic Places.

Outskirts of Ringgold on Highway 41, Catoosa County, eight miles south of the Tennessee border.

Historic Churches and Temples of Georgia

Macon and Middle Georgia

KEA'S METHODIST CHURCH, ADRIAN

Kea's Methodist Church was founded in 1820 by the Reverend Morin Key. It was rebuilt by his eldest son, Burrell, who changed the spelling of his name to Kea. He then deeded the church to the Methodists. It is the mother church of Methodism in the Adrian area.

Near Adrian, Emanuel County.

CARTER'S CHAPEL, LAURENS COUNTY

Carter's Chapel near Dublin is a fine example of a rural Georgia church built to serve a single family. The land for Carter's Chapel was donated in 1876 by John Gillis Carter, a doctor and farmer, and son of Willis and Edith Carter, the family's Georgia founders.

The first building was made of hand-sawed local lumber. Originally arriving at church on horseback and in wagons, the Carter family and their descendants have kept the chapel functioning. The membership reached a peak of more than 150 in the early 1900s, but with changing agricultural conditions and life-styles, the membership has been severely reduced since then. Yet family members and friends still gather on the first Sunday in May each year at Carter's Chapel for a reunion.

Near Dublin, Laurens County.

ST. STEPHEN'S EPISCOPAL CHURCH, MILLEDGEVILLE

The first St. Stephen's Church in Milledgeville was erected in 1843, two years after the parish of the same name was incorporated by the Georgia legislature. The building was very plain, but still fulfilled the wishes of Bishop Stephen Elliott, first bishop of Georgia, to have a parish at what was then the state capital.

The membership began growing during the Civil War, due to the influx of coastal and northern Georgians, the latter fearing destruction from Sherman's army, which ironically came through Milledgeville. The church building suffered serious damage both from enemy troops and from an explosion at the arsenal next door.

The postwar congregation was too poor to rebuild the church during Reconstruction. The structure was renovated in its present style in 1884, at which time a roof of Gothic design and a vestibule were added. In 1909 the parish received a new organ from George W. Perkins, a New Yorker. He had heard of the permanent damage done to the church organ by General Sherman's men when they poured sorghum syrup into the pipes. Since these perpetrators were attached to the 107th New York Infantry Regiment, Mr. Perkins felt his act was performed out of a sense of duty.

Today St. Stephen's Church, whose rolls have contained the names of some of Georgia's most prominent Episcopalians, continues to grow and prosper.

®On the National Register of Historic Places.

Downtown Milledgeville at 220 South Wayne Street.

MONTICELLO PRESBYTERIAN CHURCH, MONTICELLO

Monticello Presbyterian Church was organized in 1829 within the bounds of the Hopewell Presbytery, which at that time embraced a large part of Georgia and South Carolina. The first structure was erected in 1830. One of its first preachers was Samuel K. Talmage, who was also one of the founders of Oglethorpe University in Midway. Another famous minister who served Monticello Presbyterian Church was Samuel E. Axson, father of the first wife of Woodrow Wilson.

The original church building grew as the congregation grew, but it was considered unsafe after a severe windstorm caused extensive damage. So, in 1898, it was razed. The present structure was constructed that same year in a High Victorian style by Mr. Thomas Gay of Newborn, Georgia. A Sunday School annex was added in 1928.

Near the center of downtown Monticello at 210 East Washington Street.

Historic Churches and Temples of Georgia

RICHLAND BAPTIST CHURCH, TWIGGS COUNTY

Richland Baptist Church was constituted in 1811 in rural Twiggs County, which had been established only two years previously. The first church, probably a simple log structure, was built in 1813. The present building, constructed in 1844-1845, is the third one on the site. It is a classic example of the Greek Revival Style, used in many country churches in antebellum Georgia.

When the present church was built, Twiggs County plantations were becoming more prosperous, but that situation changed dramatically after the Civil War, and the church gradually lost membership. It ceased functioning in 1911, but the adjoining cemetery continued to host burials for many years after. The church is now being preserved by the Richland Restoration League, made up of descendants of the original members.

®On the National Register of Historic Places.

On Richland Church Road just south of I-16, 1.5 miles west of Highway 96, Twiggs County.

CHRIST EPISCOPAL CHURCH, MACON

Christ Episcopal Church was established in 1825, three years after the founding of Macon, by numerous early influential citizens, including Edward D. Tracy, Macon's first mayor. The congregation met in various places until 1834, when the first building, in the shape of a domed Roman Cross, was completed on the current site.

In 1851 the present building was finished, incorporating as much of the first structure as possible. The parishioners even delved through the rubble of the demolished structure for reusable bricks.

The church subsequently established missions in various parts of the Macon area, at one of which clothing was sewn for the Confederate army. The most famous wedding in the church was that of Mary Day to Sidney Lanier, Georgia's unofficial poet laureate.

Christ Church contains numerous significant artifacts. The first communion cup and bowl were retrieved from a shipwreck in the Mediterranean. They belonged to Dr. Ambrose Baber, a Maconite who was appointed chargé d'affaires to Sardinia in 1841. The organ was the first one in Macon. The pulpit is a memorial to Stephen A. Elliott, the first bishop of Georgia. The present church bell replaced the original, which was melted down for cannon during the Civil War.

®On the National Register of Historic Places.

Downtown Macon at 538 Walnut Street.

FIRST PRESBYTERIAN CHURCH, MACON

First Presbyterian Church was organized as the Presbyterian Church of Macon in 1826. In 1844 it was the host for the formation of the Synod of Georgia. The occasion was moderated by Dr. Thomas Goulding, founder of Columbia Seminary in Atlanta. His son, the Reverend Francis R. Goulding, served in the present structure, completed in 1858. He was the last minister to preach to a mixed congregation before the blacks withdrew to form the Washington Avenue Presbyterian Church in 1866. He also took over the citywide Thanksgiving service when Macon was occupied by Union forces.

First Presbyterian Church is the mother church of Tattnall Square, Vineville, and East Macon churches. A plaque in the church vestibule honors former member Sidney Lanier, Georgia's most famous poet.

®On the National Register of Historic Places.

Downtown Macon at 682 Mulberry Street.

ST. JOSEPH'S CATHOLIC CHURCH, MACON

The first recorded Christian service in Georgia was performed by a Catholic priest in DeSoto's expedition in 1540 near what is now Macon, when he baptized two Indian boys on the banks of the Ocmulgee. Later in that century a string of Indian missions was erected by Spanish Franciscans along the Georgia coast. By 1704 these missions had been destroyed by the English, who proceeded to outlaw Catholicism. It was not until after the American Revolution that Catholics again worshiped freely in Georgia.

In 1841 St. Joseph's Parish was established in Macon. From 1850 on it was served by the Diocese of Savannah. In 1887 the Jesuits began coming from New Orleans to staff St. Joseph's Parish. The next year they initiated plans to build St. Joseph's Catholic Church.

The church, built in Romanesque Neo-Gothic style, was dedicated in 1903. It is shaped like a cross and contains many striking architectural features. Among them are more than sixty stained glass windows, nearly all of which were made by master craftsmen in the Mayer Studio in Munich, Germany. The white marble used in the carvings, statues, and altars came from the Carrara quarries in Italy, which also supplied the material for Michelangelo's works. The organ, containing almost 1,000 pipes, came from Louisville, Kentucky.

®On the National Register of Historic Places.

Downtown Macon at 830 Poplar Street.

Historic Churches and Temples of Georgia

TEMPLE BETH ISRAEL, MACON

Temple Beth Israel officially began in 1859 when the Georgia legislature granted a charter to the congregation. Some of the original members came to Georgia shortly after the state was founded to escape revolutions in France and Germany.

The congregation's first regular meeting place was a rented room above a candy shop on Cherry Street. It continued to meet there until 1874, when the first Temple Beth Israel was built at Poplar and Second Streets. Meanwhile, the congregation had formed a religious school with curriculum in Hebrew, English, and German.

In 1894 the congregation became a member of the Reformed Jewish movement, and was led until 1952 by Rabbi Isaac E. Marcuson, who became a noted community and civic leader as well. The present structure was erected in 1901 at Spring and Cherry Streets and has served the Reformed Jewish community of Macon ever since.

Downtown Macon at 892 Cherry Street.

UNION UNITED METHODIST CHURCH, BUTLER

The McCant family migrated from Ireland to Charleston, South Carolina, and Virginia in the 1700s. From there, they came to Georgia and settled near Butler, where, in 1848, Sara McCant and her family founded the Union Methodist Church.

In early days, a campground was present on the church grounds, where people moved in for week-long revival meetings. Dormitories accommodated worshipers from throughout Middle Georgia.

The adjoining cemetery slightly predates the building of the church. A small wooden structure shelters the oldest grave, that of William G. D. McCant, who died in 1847 at the age of one month and eight days. A larger "house" covers George R. McCant's grave.

Descendants of Sara McCant still attend and maintain the Union United Methodist Church. The congregation, numbering around eighty, meets for worship on the fourth Sunday of every month. The Sunday School meets weekly. A fellowship hall has recently been added and refurbished with wainscoting, ceiling moldings, and a mantle from a late eighteenth-century home in South Carolina.

Near Butler, Taylor County.

ZION EPISCOPAL CHURCH, TALBOTTON

Zion Episcopal Church was erected in 1848 as a missionary church, backed financially by South Carolina rice planters. Prior to the Civil War slaves worshiped near the choir loft while whites worshiped below.

The original style of the building, which has remained unaltered, is Tudor Gothic, typical of rural English parish churches in the mid-nineteenth century. The entire building is made from wooden pegs and handmade iron nails. Many features of the interior, including the altar and the lectern pulpit, are also handmade from native walnut. The 1850 organ is still used and is operated by a hand pump.

In Talbotton on Highway 80, Talbot County.

®On the National Register of Historic Places.

CHAPEL, WARM SPRINGS

Warm Springs began as a resort area because of the presence of natural springs there. The Meriwether Inn and Guest Cottages were built to accommodate visitors from various parts of the country. The most famous visitor and resident was, undoubtedly, Franklin D. Roosevelt, who suffered from poliomyelitis. Mr. Roosevelt first went to Warm Springs in 1924 to test the reported healing powers of the waters. He subsequently built his own cottage there, known later as the "Little White House," where he died in 1945 while still president.

Mr. Roosevelt was also instrumental in founding the Georgia Warm Springs Foundation in 1927, to treat the victims of poliomyelitis, then known as infantile paralysis. The foundation supported the inn, springs, and guest cottages. As the foundation grew, new buildings were added, including the chapel in 1937. It was founded primarily by Miss Georgia M. Wilkins, a former owner of the Meriwether Inn and springs.

Today chapel services are conducted by chaplains of the Protestant, Catholic, and Jewish faiths for patients and employees of the Georgia Warm Springs Foundation, which is now run by the state of Georgia. The foundation has expanded to undertake physical and vocational rehabilitation of people suffering from various medical disorders.

At Warm Springs Foundation in Warm Springs, off Highway Alt. 27, Meriwether County.

UNITED METHODIST CHURCH, MOUNTVILLE

Mountville United Methodist Church was organized in 1828 as Mount Pleasant Methodist Church. Its first church building was a log cabin built in that year. In 1854 it became part of the Greenville circuit and later of the Hogansville circuit. In 1908 the church was moved to its present site and a new white frame building of English Gothic style was erected. The name was then changed to its present one. Over the years a parsonage, Sunday School, organ, chimes, and eleven stained glass windows have been added, the last having been installed in 1985 above the minister's pulpit. In 1985 lightning struck the bell tower and destroyed part of it. It has since been repaired to its original condition.

In Mountville, on Highway 109, seven miles east of LaGrange, Troup County.

MOUNTVILLE PRESBYTERIAN CHURCH, MOUNTVILLE

In Mountville, a few blocks off Highway 109.

Mountville Presbyterian Church was organized in 1887 as a result of a "protracted meeting," a popular type of gathering in the nineteenth century that involved days and weeks of intensive preaching and worship. Soon after the founding, the First Mountville Presbyterian Church was built, a simple wooden structure so poorly constructed that it soon leaned. Supposedly, children ran by it "for fear it would fall." It lasted, however, until about 1907, when the present building replaced it. The new building was constructed of granite from the Mountville quarry and was in the English Gothic style with a buttressed tower on the left.

In the early twentieth century, the membership grew to 75, but diminished after that. From 1954 to 1976 the church was open only for special summertime revival services, mainly through the efforts of a few descendants of the original charter members, especially Esther Fincher of Decatur. She and her family are the last surviving members of the church, which has been closed completely since 1976.

FIRST BAPTIST CHURCH, LAGRANGE

The First Baptist Church of LaGrange was organized in 1828. At the time, LaGrange was only a small village. In fact, the first Baptist church building, presumably of logs, was so primitive that hogs once disrupted services while digging for roots under it.

Both blacks and whites worshiped in the church, and continued to do so after the present building was completed in 1859. After the Civil War, however, the blacks withdrew to form their own Baptist congregation.

During the war the church basement was used as a Confederate hospital. In 1865 a group of women "homeguards" called "the Nancy Harts" confronted Wilson's Raiders as they entered LaGrange. They surrendered when promised that the city would be saved from destruction, thus sparing many buildings, including the First Baptist Church.

Two major enlargements of the church occurred in 1922 and 1937, giving it its present appearance.

On Lafayette Square, 100 Broad Street, LaGrange.

BETH-EL SYNAGOGUE, LAGRANGE

Beth-El Synagogue was originally built around 1880 as a church for the Episcopalians in LaGrange. In the 1940s it became a synagogue with thirty to forty members. The synagogue continues to serve the small Jewish community of LaGrange, while the building's original architecture remains essentially intact.

Church Street, LaGrange.

IDA CASON CALLAWAY MEMORIAL CHAPEL, PINE MOUNTAIN

Ida Cason Callaway Memorial Chapel is located next to Falls Creek in the midst of Callaway Gardens, a combination resort and nature study area. Callaway Gardens, nationally famous for its beauty, was founded by Cason J. Callaway in 1954. He built the chapel in 1962 to provide a place for visitors to meditate and worship. He named it for his mother, Ida Cason Callaway.

The chapel's design is English Gothic, in the tradition of sixteenth- and seventeenth-century rural chapels. The roof is made of slate from Vermont. The remainder of the materials, however, are native to Georgia. The walls are made of quartzite fieldstone, the beams of red oak, and the floors of Cherokee flagstone. Stained glass windows showing scenes from nature are also present, with four of them representing the seasons of the year as they appear at Callaway Gardens. The chapel has no regular worship service, but it is used for small weddings. The chapel's Möller pipe organ is used for concerts throughout the year.

Although the Callaway Chapel is much newer than the other structures in this book, it is still of significant historical value. It was built by a private individual for use by the public as a non-denominational chapel. Also, it serves as a retreat in an area that is used not only as a resort but as a huge botanical garden that has been nurtured and preserved through the efforts of one philanthropic family.

In Callaway Gardens, Highway Alt. 27, Harris County.

HAMILTON BAPTIST CHURCH, HAMILTON

Hamilton Baptist Church is part of the Columbus Baptist Association, which was organized in 1829 at Mulberry Grove, ten miles from Hamilton. Twelve churches from Talbot, Harris, and Muscogee counties made up the Association. Hamilton Baptist Church, which was first known as Baptist Church of Christ, Lebanon, has no records prior to 1865, as they were burned in a federal raid at that time.

The present church building was completed in 1890 and was dedicated by Mercer University's president, Dr. G. A. Nunnalee, on 21 September of that year. That day is considered one of the most important in the church's history because nearly enough money was taken in at collection to pay off the indebtedness of the building. Over the years, Hamilton Baptist Church has shared its pastor with Waverly Hall and Cataula churches, thereby serving many Baptists in and around the Hamilton area.

®On the National Register of Historic Places.

In Hamilton, Harris County, Highway Alt. 27.

Columbus and South Georgia

FIRST PRESBYTERIAN CHURCH, COLUMBUS

Early in 1830, the First Presbyterian Church of Columbus was organized by a band of fourteen men and women under the direction of their pastor, the Reverend John Baker of Savannah. He was one of fifty Presbyterian ministers who went out from the Midway Church to preach. Services were originally held in the courthouse until a church was erected in 1831 at the corner of Second Avenue and Eighth Street. It was later moved to Second Avenue and Tenth Street, where a larger structure replaced it in 1845.

The third and present church building was dedicated in 1862. Its plans and specifications were procured from the architect of the Presbyterian Church Board of Church Erection in Philadelphia, Pennsylvania. They were amended by members of the local building committee for the new church before work was begun.

For many years a mission school was conducted each Sunday afternoon in the Sunday School room of the church. The pupils for this school were mainly from the factory tenements, known as factory boarding houses, which were located in the areas around the textile mills. Many in the mission school reportedly made their first acquaintance with the alphabet there, learning to read from the school's well-stocked library. When the old factory boarding houses were abandoned and torn down, the mission school ceased to exist.

The church was partially destroyed by fire in 1891, but the exterior was virtually undamaged except for the roof. While the church was being rebuilt, the congregation rented the Old Trinity Episcopal church building across the street. The rebuilding effort took exactly one year, at which time regular services were resumed.

®On the National Register of Historic Places.

Downtown Columbus at 1100 First Avenue.

TRINITY EPISCOPAL CHURCH, COLUMBUS

Trinity Episcopal Church was organized in 1834, six years after the founding of Columbus. The first building, completed in 1835 and damaged by fire in 1847, was nevertheless used until 1891, when the present English Country Gothic structure was erected. The church, along with the Tudor Gothic parish house built in 1925, has served the Episcopalian community of Columbus on a continuing basis.

®On the National Register of Historic Places.

Trinity Episcopal Church has also served many of the civic and cultural needs of the entire community. In addition to helping to start St. Thomas, the other local Episcopal church, Trinity Episcopal Church also founded Trinity School in 1951. The latter has since become Brookstone School, an independent college preparatory institution. The church has sponsored Vietnamese refugees, furnished clothing for foster children, and helped to support a girls' home.

Downtown Columbus at 1130 First Avenue.

ST. LUKE UNITED METHODIST CHURCH, COLUMBUS

St. Luke United Methodist Church and Columbus were established in the same year (1828), ranking it as the city's oldest congregation. In 1978 it celebrated its sesquicentennial, spanning a period in which it had seen eighty-nine pastors and associates and six different buildings.

The first Methodist "Society" was organized in 1825 by the Reverend Andrew Hammill and was comprised of fifty-four white and seven black members. Hammill was a preacher for the Columbus Methodist congregation and was a missionary to the Indians. The first worship service by the city's fledgling Methodist congregation was held in the open under brush arbors and later in a rough log building at the corner of Broad and 11th Streets. The Methodists built their first church on the southern half of a city block granted by the Georgia legislature for religious purposes. The Baptists, who organized in 1829, occupied the northern half, where they erected their first house of worship the following year. The second Methodist church structure was completed in 1836, and had the distinction of being the first brick Methodist church in Georgia. In 1844 St. Luke sided with other Southern churches in the dispute over the slavery issue, which led to the split of the Methodist Church into Southern and Northern branches. After the schism, the local congregation continued to grow, and a new, larger building of classical Greek style was completed in 1847. An even larger one was built in 1900, but burned on Mother's Day in 1942. The present Georgian style sanctuary was dedicated on Mother's Day, 1948.

In 1840 the Womens's Society of St. Luke organized the city's oldest benevolent institution, now known as the Ann Elizabeth Shepherd Home. In 1844 Mrs. Seaborn Jones, then Society president, was instrumental in helping to establish the Columbus Female Orphan Asylum.

Downtown Columbus at 1104 Second Avenue.

®On the National Register of Historic Places.

OLD ST. MARK UNITED METHODIST CHURCH, COLUMBUS

Prior to 1865 no history of St. Mark United Methodist Church is available. In that year, it was known as Wesley Chapel Church and was located on the banks of the Chattahoochee River, where the Eagle and Phenix Mill now stands. When the mill purchased the property in 1873, Mr. George Swift donated a lot on Broad Street where a second church was built the next year. It was known as the Broad Street Church and was used until 1902, when the property was sold and the present location on Third Avenue was obtained. In 1913 the name was changed to Methodist Tabernacle and in 1914, to St. Mark. In 1974 St. Mark United Methodist once again moved, this time to an area outside the downtown district of Columbus. The Third Avenue church was sold and subsequently became a day care center.

®On the National Register of Historic Places.

Downtown Columbus at 1605 Third Avenue.

Columbus and South Georgia

FIRST BAPTIST CHURCH, COLUMBUS

The First Baptist Church of Columbus was organized on Valentine's Day in 1829 by twelve people, one of whom was a slave. It was originally called Ephesus Baptist Church of Christ. The first church, a frame building, was erected in 1830 on land granted by the state of Georgia. It was later moved to another location to be used as a city mission station. Two subsequent larger churches were built in 1841 and 1859, the latter being the present structure. A Sunday School was added in 1924, and in the 1940s a new chapel was also built. The latter was built to add classrooms as well as to take care of

Boy Scouts and recreational facilities. Still further additions were made in 1984, reflecting the continuing growth of the congregation.

The bell shown in the painting was installed in 1859, the year the present sanctuary was built. It consists of 1,201 pounds of brass and silver, the latter being legal tender donated by church members. In 1896, during remodeling, the bell was loaned to Rose Hill Baptist Church, then fifty years later to Benning Hills Baptist Church. It was returned in 1963. The excep-

tional stained glass windows, installed in 1894, are perhaps the most significant features of the church.

One of many outstanding members of the First Baptist Church was J. Albert Kirven, a descendant of one of the twelve organizers. A noted civic leader, he helped promote the building of the downtown Columbus YMCA and served as its president for eighteen years. The building, a gift of philanthropist George Foster Peabody, is thought to be the only YMCA in the county made from marble.

®On the National Register of Historic Places.

Downtown Columbus at 212 12th Street.

CHURCH OF THE HOLY FAMILY, COLUMBUS

In 1828, when the city of Columbus was laid out, a square block was given to the Baptists and Methodists, on which they built churches that are represented elsewhere in the book. In 1832 after the legislature was petitioned by the local Catholics and Presbyterians, a smaller block was ceded to these groups. Although the Presbyterians never used the land, the Catholics built a church and rectory in 1835 on present day Chapel Street. The church, known as Saints Philip and James, sent missionaries to Georgia, Florida, and Alabama during the pre-Civil War years.

In 1862 a band of Sisters of Mercy arrived from St. Augustine, Florida, to escape from federal gunboats and founded St. Joseph's Academy. They subsequently donated the rose garden adjacent to their school for construction of a new church, which was completed in 1880 and was renamed Church of the Holy Family. The original church was razed, but the rectory was spared and moved to lower Broadway. It is presently being used by an Episcopalian congregation.

®On the National Register of Historic Places.

Downtown Columbus at 320 12th Street.

ST. JAMES A.M.E. CHURCH, COLUMBUS

St. James A.M.E. Church in Columbus ranks as the second oldest church of its denomination in Georgia, St. Philip in Savannah being the oldest. The first recorded pastor was the Reverend William Gaines, who served in 1864, a year after St. James was organized.

The property on which the church is located was granted to the A.M.E. church by the Georgia legislature in 1873. The present edifice was begun in 1875 and completed in 1876. The tower was added in 1886. The building is of frame construction with exterior walls of solid masonry and handmade bricks. According to a historical sketch from the church bulletin, the front doors came from Asbury Methodist Episcopal Church, which was built for slaves, and are probably the oldest parts of St. James Church.

®On the National Register of Historic Places.

Downtown Columbus at 1002 Sixth Avenue.

ST. JOHN A.M.E. CHURCH, COLUMBUS

St. John A.M.E. Church is the outgrowth of its mother church, St. James A.M.E. Church of Columbus. The church sanctuary itself was built in 1870 on land donated by an organization of white women, who specified that a house of worship be built on it. The original building was wooden and was called St. John Chapel, but was later renamed St. John A.M.E. Church.

The present brick structure is in the Victorian Gothic style, with a round tower and conical roof that are unique to Columbus. Numerous renovations have taken place over the years, including the addition of a basement in 1890. In 1923 a pipe organ was installed, making St. John A.M.E. Church the first black church in Columbus to achieve this distinction. Over the years many prominent professionals as well as highly respected civic and business leaders have attended St. John A.M.E. Church.

®On the National Register of Historic Places.

Downtown Columbus at 1516 Fifth Avenue.

FIRST AFRICAN BAPTIST CHURCH AND PARSONAGE, COLUMBUS

First African Baptist Church of Columbus was organized in 1840. The present structure of medieval architecture is the third one built by the church and was erected in 1915. The first church was of frame construction and was destroyed by fire. The second one was brick and was built in 1881. First African Baptist was the church where Ma Rainey, Columbus native and famed "Mother of the Blues," was baptized.

Like its counterpart, St. James A.M.E.

Church, First African Baptist Church has produced some of the city's most outstanding black leaders. Perhaps the best known of these was the Reverend T. W. Smith, who assumed the pastorate in 1938 as the church was struggling to recover from the Great Depression. Rev. Smith is well remembered for his community service, as well as his spiritual leadership. He organized the first black Boy Scout troop in Muscogee County in 1940. He was a chaplain at City

Hospital, and, in 1945, he succeeded in organizing the county's first black Girl Scout troop. Selma University awarded him an honorary Doctor of Divinity degree in 1945.

Over the years First African Baptist Church has seen many renovations and additions, including the establishment of a day care center across the street that functioned from 1968 to 1980. The church continues in active service to this day.

Downtown Columbus at 901 Fifth Avenue.

®On the National Register of Historic Places.

THE INFANTRY CENTER CHAPEL, FT. BENNING

On the main post, Ft. Benning.

The Infantry Center Chapel, built in 1934 and 1935, was one of the earliest permanent structures at Ft. Benning, constructed at the same time as what was then the post head-quarters and the officers' club. It was de-signed by the well-known Atlanta architectural firm of Hentz, Adler and Shutze (which also designed the The Tem-ple in Atlanta). It was modeled after St. John's Episcopal Church in Charleston, South Carolina.

This interdenominational chapel has a num-ber of unique features. Among the ten stained glass windows is one that shows the "Follow Me" flags from the Infantry Center and another is the crest for the U. S. Army Chaplain School. Also, ten flags flank the al-tar, representing the colors of ten retired regiments.

The "Liberty Carillon," a gift of Harvey S. Firestone, Jr. has an accompanying citation from 1946 which reads, "This beautiful voice has been enjoyed by 600,000 officers and enlisted men enroute overseas and by 850,000 returnees. The spiritual appreciation was truly amazing. Its wartime job glo-riously done."

PROVIDENCE UNITED METHODIST CHURCH, STEWART COUNTY

Providence United Methodist Church is located in Providence Canyon, the "Little Grand Canyon," so called because of its similarity to the world-famous geological phenomenon. The first church was built in 1833 as a log cabin on land donated by the Reverend David Walker Lowe for the purpose of establishing a church and school (Providence Academy). Lowe was a Methodist circuit rider in both South Carolina and Georgia. The land where the old church was located is between two of the canyons. The present structure was built on the old Lumpkin-Florence road. The church's cemetery contains the remains of many early Stewart County residents, including the Reverend Lowe.

Providence Canyon State Park, west of Lumpkin.

CHURCH ROW, LOUVALE

Louvale Church Row consists of approximately four acres of land on which are situated four wooden frame buildings—three churches and one school—as well as a small cemetery. The churches are New Hope Baptist, Louvale (formerly Marvin) United Methodist, and Antioch Primitive Baptist, with which the school is associated. All the churches are examples of late nineteenth-century rural Georgia church architecture. The school is a two-room structure, typical of the same period.

The Baptists in Stewart County first worshiped in Richland. However, in 1839 Anti-

Columbus and South Georgia

och Church was built to serve the members living at a distance from Richland. In 1851 the entire congregation moved to the present site, two miles north of the original one. There they worshiped in a log building until the present church and school were built, possibly in the 1870s. In 1895 the school was sold to the Stewart County Board of Education. In 1899 and in the very early 1900s, Marvin (Louvale) Methodist and Louvale Baptist churches, respectively, were built adjacent to Antioch Baptist Church, which was meticulously restored by members of the congregation in the mid-1980s.

On Highway 27, Stewart County, 28 miles south of Columbus.

EBENEZER BAPTIST CHURCH, LUMPKIN

®On the National Register of Historic Places.

Ebenezer Baptist Church was originally Lumpkin Methodist Church, built in 1857. In 1913 it was given to the Baptists and acquired its present name. At that time, it was taken apart, moved from uptown Lumpkin to its present site, and reassembled. It is no longer in use and is in need of repairs, but renovation is planned.

Near the Lumpkin town square on Troutman Road (toward Westville).

OLD DAMASCUS METHODIST CHURCH
AND CLIMAX PRESBYTERIAN CHURCH, WESTVILLE

Westville, the inspiration of historian Joseph Mahan, is the recreation of a functioning 1850 Georgia community. Started in 1968, it now contains more than thirty authentic structures and serves as a tourist attraction as well as an educational tool for children and adults alike. In 1976 presidential candidate Jimmy Carter was the main speaker at the celebration of America's bicentennial held there.

Two churches are a part of Westville. One is Climax Presbyterian, named for the town where it was located before being moved to Westville. The church building was dedicated in 1851, and was first called Curry's Church, then Mineral Springs Church, before acquiring its present name in 1891. Climax Presbyterian was organized by the Florida Presbytery and transferred to one in Georgia in 1868. In 1970 the congregation merged with the Bainbridge Presbyterian Church, and the Climax Church was given to Westville, where it represents a typical church building of the time and the area.

The other church, Old Damascus Methodist, was built in 1879. It was an active church until about 1911, when it was sold into private hands and was subsequently used as a grain storage barn. It is highly valued by Westville because of its unique interior. Its walls and ceiling are decorated with paintings of the Italian Renaissance Revival style. The belief is that the art work was done by an itinerant painter because it is probably too sophisticated to be local folk art. The paintings now show stippling caused by soot tracks from a kerosene lantern. Since the building is too new to meet the strict criterion for inclusion in Westville proper, it is located just outside the gates, where it will be used as an orientation center after its restoration.

WESTVILLE'S DAMASCUS CHURCH UNDER RESTORATION

Westville is on Troutman Road, one mile south of Lumpkin.

RICHLAND METHODIST CHURCH, RICHLAND

The Richland Methodist Church was founded around 1840, but was later disbanded. It was reorganized in 1888. A wooden building was used for worship at that time.

The present brick church was built in 1912, using the design of architect Thomas W. Smith, Sr. Smith, a leading architect throughout the Southeast, was the senior partner in the firm of T. W. and E. O. Smith. In 1912 he helped organize the first association of architects in Georgia, and served as its president until it later became the Georgia State Board for the Examination and Registration of Architects. He was then appointed by Governor Hardwick to serve on the Board. In addition to the Richland Methodist Church, he also built Trinity Episcopal Church in Columbus and a church in Clayton, Georgia, identical to the one in Richland.

Downtown Richland on Hamilton Avenue.

®Pending listing on the National Register of Historic Places, 1986.

HARMONY PRIMITIVE BAPTIST CHURCH, RICHLAND

Harmony Primitive Baptist Church was constituted in 1839 when a few people met at the home of Whitington Wiggins for that purpose. They built a little wooden church and eventually added a shelter on the back for the black members of the community who did not have a church of their own.

Around 1894 a new church building was constructed in the same location and of the same architecture as the original. Members from other small rural churches in the area attended occasionally and they all shared the services of a minister. Although five members of the congregation remain, the church has not been used for services in several years. Nevertheless, the building has been well cared for and the adjoining cemetery is still used for burials.

Ponder Street on the outskirts of Richland.

SHILOH MARION BAPTIST CHURCH, MARION COUNTY

Shiloh Marion Baptist Church is the last remaining structure of the once substantial community of Church Hill in rural Marion County. The settlement, then on the federal road from Columbus to St. Marys, was founded in 1828. The community took its name from the five churches, including Shiloh Marion Baptist, that were present there. The other denominations were Free Will Baptist, Methodist, Presbyterian, and Christian Union.

®On the National Register of Historic Places.

Shiloh Marion Baptist Church itself was built around 1835, and together with its cemetery is a good example of a simple rural antebellum Georgia churchyard, with simplicity of detail and lack of ornamentation. It appears to reflect both the attitudes and the lack of wealth of rural Georgians of that time. Since most people in Church Hill were farmers and had little money, they often piled the Shiloh Marion minister's buggy with corn meal, home grown flour, syrup, hickory smoked hams, fruits, and vegetables in lieu of cash.

Georgia Highway 41 at Marion-Webster County line.

Columbus and South Georgia

ANDREW CHAPEL UNITED METHODIST CHURCH, SCHLEY COUNTY

In 1860 a group of individuals residing in Schley County recognized the need for a place to worship. They constructed a brush arbor near the present site of Andrew Chapel Church south of Ellaville. The Reverend Dennis O'Sriscal was the first pastor, serving from 1860 to 1861.

In 1871 Charnel Bell Strange and his wife Nancy Elizabeth Goodson deeded a plot of land for the purpose of establishing a church with the stipulation that a cemetery was never to be placed on the lot. It is be-lieved that the church was named for Bishop James O. Andrew, who was the presiding bishop of the South Georgia Methodist Conference during the organization of the church.

The interior of the church was renovated in 1915, when the Corinthian columns were added to the exterior. In 1980 the Mountain Springs Methodist Church, which was located in Macon County, was purchased and moved to the site and became "Little Andrew" fellowship hall.

US Highway 19, just south of Ellaville.

ST. JAMES PENNINGTON CHURCH, ANDERSONVILLE

St. James Pennington Church was built in 1927 out of native fieldstone and hand-hewn cypress logs. It originally stood on property three miles southeast of Andersonvile on land deeded to the Episcopal Diocese of Georgia by the Pennington family.

The church was in continuous use until 1947, when Dr. James Lawrance, the original rector, died. He had manually helped with the construction of the church and had donated hundreds of books for a free lending library. After his death, the church stood unused but often visited until 1975, when it was moved to the Andersonville National Historic Site and was restored, a further gift of the Pennington family. Some of its finest features include hand-forged iron sconces and candelabras by Jay Reakirt, Andersonville's Pioneer Farm blacksmith.

Today, the church is open daily and available for small weddings. No services are held there except for an annual nondenominational ceremony during the Andersonville Historic Fair.

DEATH
BEFORE
DISHONOR

NEW JERSEY

Andersonville National Historic Site is on Georgia Highway 49, 21 miles northeast of Plains.

Historic Churches and Temples of Georgia

AMERICUS PRESBYTERIAN CHURCH, AMERICUS

The Americus Presbyterian Church was organized in 1842, and the first church building was erected in 1851. When it later burned, the location of the next church was changed. The second building was in use during the Civil War and (allegedly) witnessed an interesting event. When General Sherman invaded Americus, the custodian of a silver pot and two silver goblets used for services feared for their safety. She took them to an out-of-town friend, who buried them until the danger was over. After the war they were returned, providing many more years of use.

The present structure, completed in 1884, is Gothic Victorian. The church bell is the original. It has had not only the traditional use of calling for morning services, but was also the fire bell for the nearby fire department for a time. During the Iran hostage crisis of 1979 through 1981, it rang daily at noon as a reminder of the captives.

Downtown Americus at 125 South Jackson Street.

ST. ANDREW'S LUTHERAN CHURCH, PLAINS

The present St. Andrew's Lutheran Church is the result of a merger in 1966 of St. Andrew's and St. Mark's Lutheran Church of Botsford, five miles southwest of Plains.

St. Mark's Church was started in 1870 by a group of Lutherans from South Carolina. About ten years later "Plains of Dura" was established around a railroad station, and it grew as Botsford declined. So the congregation of St. Mark's voted in 1905 to build a church in Plains. St. Andrew's was built in 1907 with members of St. Mark's assisting in the actual construction, including the making of "rock-like" blocks. A parsonage was built in 1947 and a parish house was added in 1952.

St. Mark's continued to meet as a congregation until the merger in 1966. St. Mark's church building and cemetery are all that remain of Botsford. Lutheran congregations have also existed in the parish over the years in Magnolia Springs, Brownwood, and Americus, but none has survived.

®On the National Register of Historic Places.

Downtown Plains on North Bond Street.

PLAINS BAPTIST CHURCH, PLAINS

The Plains Baptist Church originated as the
Lebanon Baptist Church in 1848 on what is
the present site of the Lebanon Cemetery.
In the 1870s it gave financial support to a
missionary to the Creek Indians and to the
Georgia Baptist Children's Home.

In 1889 the church was moved to Plains,
and in 1906 the present building was
erected. Over the years the congregation,
which has grown from its original twenty

®On the National Register of Historic Places.

members to nearly three hundred in the small town of Plains, has continued to support causes such as the Children's Home and missionaries throughout the world.

The Plains Baptist church has the singular distinction in the state of Georgia of having a former president of the United ̲̲̲ an ordained de̲̲̲ tize̲̲̲ Sun̲̲̲

Downtown Plains on South Bond Street.

OLD MOUNT HOREB BAPTIST CHURCH, SYLVESTER

Mount Horeb Church was built in 1848 along the banks of the Flint River near Pindertown, Worth County (then Dooley County). It was constructed on land ceded to the government of the United States by the Creek Indians in 1821.

The church was moved to its present site in 1868, but ceased functioning about 1901 because of a lack of membership. However, a small group of descendants of the original members meets yearly to preserve the church and cemetery, as well as the original cemetery near Pindertown.

Approximately fifteen miles northeast of Albany and 2.7 miles east of Highway 300, four-mile marker in Worth County.

LEESBURG PRESBYTERIAN CHURCH, LEESBURG

Leesburg Presbyterian Church was established in 1869. The first church building was constructed in 1872, the present one in 1906. The fellowship hall was added in 1978. Although the membership has always been small, and at the present time numbers only seventy, the church has been very well cared for. It presently has its first full-time minister.

Highway 19 in Lee County, north of Albany.

ST. TERESA'S CATHOLIC CHURCH, ALBANY

St. Teresa's Church was built on land deeded to the Catholics in 1859 by Colonel Nelson Tift, founder of Albany. The church was built in the style of other frontier and small mission churches popular at that time. The exterior was completed in 1860 from bricks handmade by laborers on the S. L. Barbour Plantation, but the interior work was temporarily interrupted by the Civil War, during which time the building was used as a Confederate hospital. Regular mass was first celebrated in 1875, and the church was dedicated in 1882, under the patronage of St. Teresa of Avila, Spain.

In 1902, the same year stained glass windows and the ceiling were installed, St. Teresa's became the center of the largest Catholic mission area in the United States. It covered all of southwest Georgia and served in that capacity until 1958, when a new parish church was built. The original building still holds mass once a week, making it both the oldest church building in Albany and the oldest Catholic church in Georgia still in use.

Downtown Albany at 315 Residence Avenue.

®On the National Register of Historic Places.

ALL SAINTS EPISCOPAL CHURCH, THOMASVILLE

All Saints Episcopal Church is unique among churches in this book in that it was originally both of a different denomination and at a different location. It was built in 1882 on its original site as St. Augustine's Roman Catholic Church. It was deconsecrated in the late 1960s when a new Roman Catholic church was built elsewhere in the city.

The land with the church on it was purchased for business reasons by a local attorney in 1973. Rather than tear the building down, he gave it to the Thomasville Landmark Organization in 1980. It was moved the next year to property owned by the All Saints Episcopal Church Mission in the Tockwotton district. Also on the property was a two-story building and a warehouse, which were converted into a rectory and parish house, respectively. The church was consecrated on All Saints Day, 1982, by Bishop Paul Reaves, bishop of Georgia, and it became a parish in 1983.

®On the National Register of Historic Places.

Tockwotton district of Thomasville.

BETHANY CONGREGATIONAL CHURCH, THOMASVILLE

®On the National Register of Historic Places.

Bethany Congregational Church was founded in 1891 to serve the needs of Allen Normal and Industrial School, one of the earliest private institutions for blacks in south Georgia. Although the school was closed in 1933, the church continues to serve the community. Among the many ministers who have served the church with distinction is the Reverend Andrew Young, who has gained national prominence as a civil rights activist, United Nations Ambassador under President Jimmy Carter, and mayor of Atlanta.

In Thomasville at 1122 Lester Street.

SPRINGHILL METHODIST CHURCH, THOMAS COUNTY

The first church in Thomas County was a log cabin built without sawed lumber or nails around 1822, in the area called Springhill. The congregation rapidly outgrew the initial structure, which was replaced by the present one in 1833. At that time quarterly camp meetings were held there, attracting people in covered wagons from many counties in south Georgia and north Florida. The biggest event was Muster Day, an annual Fourth of July barbecue and celebration.

As other churches appeared in the area, Springhill Church gradually lost its active membership and today has only quarterly meetings, conducted by Methodist speakers. Some of the graves in the church's cemetery are reportedly those of slaves, indicating that both black and white churches of Thomas County had their beginnings at Springhill.

South of Thomasville near Metcalf Road in the Springhill area.